# STREETS OF MOGADISHU

Leadership At Its Best,
Political Correctness
At Its Worst!

*Jim & Alicia –*

## COL (Ret.) Danny McKnight
## U.S. Army

*Danny R McKnight*

*God Bless USA!*

**LEADING**
**FOR FREEDOM**
WWW.LEADINGFORFREEDOM.COM

LEADING FOR FREEDOM
Chester, Maryland, USA
www.leadingforfreedom.com


First Edition: July 2011

Editors: Adam Davies
Mary Hogan Hearle

Book and cover design: Kathleen Lawyer Dodson
Background cover photo: Jose Cendon
Map base: U.S. Defense Mapping Agency
Map art: Leading For Freedom
Photos: U.S. Army Rangers
Introduction photo: MSG Robert R. Hargreaves Jr.



ISBN: 978-0-615-51164-1
Library of Congress Control Number: 2011934095


Printed in the United States of America

This writing is a tribute to all members of Task Force RANGER. Each one will always be a hero to me.

My special dedication is to the seventeen Task Force RANGER soldiers who made the ultimate sacrifice in October 1993, and also to their loved ones. Rest in peace, brave warriors.

I also want to honor the memory of two more of my Rangers from the Task Force: 1SG Glenn Harris and CWO Aaron Weaver (SGT Weaver in 1993). Both survived the battle of October 3, 1993, but later died serving our country elsewhere. To them and their loved ones, your sacrifice will never be forgotten.

# Contents

# "One Nation Under God"

Greater love hath no man than this, that a man lay down his life for his friend.

*John 15:13*

*Your courage, bravery, sacrifice for country and freedom will never be forgotten.*

MSG Gary Gordon

SFC Randy Shughart

SSG Daniel Busch

SFC Earl Fillmore

SFC Matt Rierson

MSG Tim Martin

CPL Jamie Smith

SGT Casey Joyce

SPC Richard Kowalewski, Jr.

SGT Dominick Pilla

SGT Lorenzo Ruiz

CPL James Cavaco

SSG William Cleveland

SSG Thomas Field

CW4 Raymond Frank

CW4 Clifton Wolcott

CW3 Donovan Briley

SGT Cornell Houston

PFC James Martin

# THE RANGER CREED

**R**ecognizing that I volunteered as a Ranger, fully knowing the hazards of my chosen profession, I will always endeavor to uphold the prestige, honor, and high esprit de corps of my Ranger Regiment.

**A**cknowledging the fact that a Ranger is a more elite soldier who arrives at the cutting edge of battle by land, sea, or air, I accept the fact that as a Ranger my country expects me to move farther, faster and fight harder than any other soldier.

**N**ever shall I fail my comrades. I will always keep myself mentally alert, physically strong and morally straight and I will shoulder more than my share of the task whatever it may be. One-hundred-percent and then some.

**G**allantly will I show the world that I am a specially selected and well trained soldier. My courtesy to superior officers, neatness of dress and care of equipment shall set the example for others to follow.

**E**nergetically will I meet the enemies of my country. I shall defeat them on the field of battle for I am better trained and will fight with all my might. Surrender is not a Ranger word. I will never leave a fallen comrade to fall into the hands of the enemy and under no circumstances will I ever embarrass my country.

**R**eadily will I display the intestinal fortitude required to fight on to the Ranger objective and complete the mission though I be the lone survivor.

**RANGERS LEAD THE WAY!**

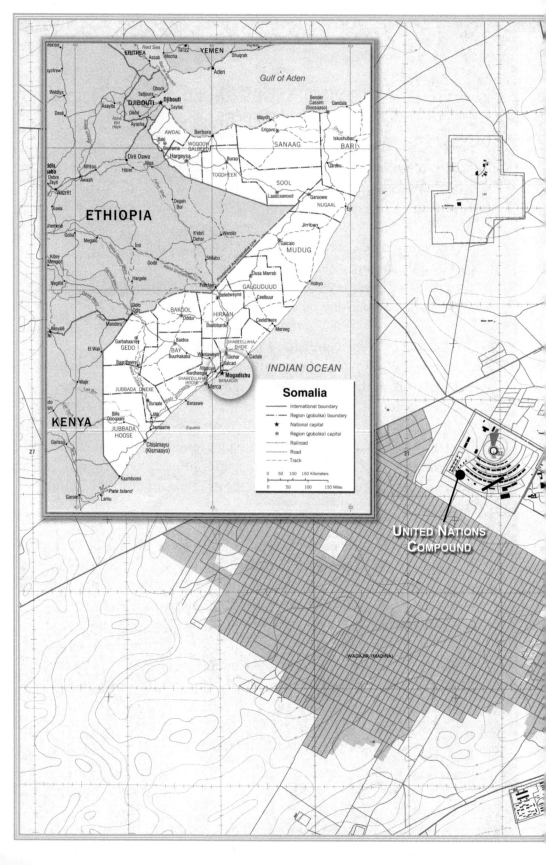

### Somalia

| | |
|---|---|
| —————— | International boundary |
| —·—·— | Region (*gobolka*) boundary |
| ★ | National capital |
| ◉ | Region (*gobolka*) capital |
| ┼┼┼┼ | Railroad |
| —————— | Road |
| — — — | Track |

0   50   100   150 Kilometers

0   50   100   150 Miles

**UNITED NATIONS COMPOUND**

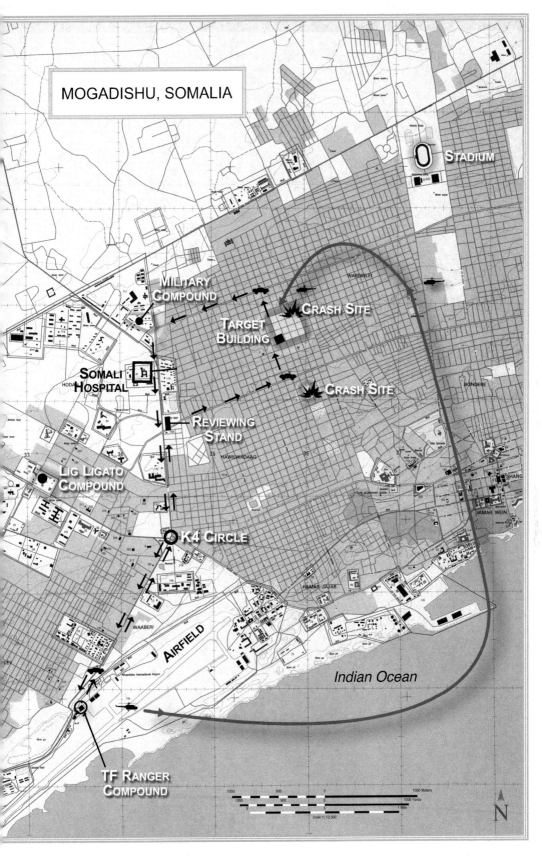

# Introduction

At approximately 3:40 on Sunday afternoon, October 3, 1993, the assault was initiated, and within twenty minutes the prisoners were under control of the assaulting Delta Force personnel. This operation into the most dangerous part of Mogadishu was almost finished, or so it seemed. Unfortunately, things changed very quickly and the men of Task Force RANGER would become involved in the most intense combat situation for American troops since the Vietnam War.

This writing addresses not only this situation, commonly referred to as the Battle of the Black Sea or Black Hawk Down, but also the untold stories of that military engagement, from leadership to the impacts of politics on military decisions, to various aspects of combat operations in Mogadishu by Task Force RANGER.

The discussion of leadership and decision-making incorporates all levels of military service, from the Commander-in-Chief (President) down to the Sergeants in the Task Force. It provides the reader with a better understanding of the privilege associated with leading our American soldiers. This book describes leadership in what can best be called leading during the best and worst of times … the best is seeing American soldiers perform in combat far beyond any normal expectation, while the worst is seeing how combat can involve

American soldiers making the ultimate sacrifice for a comrade and their country. This reality of sacrifice is not new by any means; our great country's existence is based on sacrifice that began over two hundred thirty-five years ago. Our nation has been confronted with many difficult challenges along the way, and we have survived them all primarily due to unwavering leadership and the willingness of American patriots to sacrifice their lives.

This writing also deals with the subject of hard decision-making in military operations, especially in combat operations. Simply stated, it is the soldier-leader on the ground who makes the life or death decision in combat operations like those encountered in the streets of Mogadishu in 1993. Yes, the soldier-leader who is at the tip of the spear makes the most critical decisions, not the politician sitting in the easy chair in the air-conditioned office in Washington, D.C.

The mission to Somalia in 1993 was a three-phased operation focused clearly on capturing Mohamed Farah Aidid. It was to be accomplished by a Special Operations Task Force commanded by Major General William Garrison. The organization became known as Task Force RANGER, composed of superb military units with outstanding leaders and soldiers who were trained and ready to accomplish the mission—the best of the best.

There are many superb writings already in print about the events of October 1993 in Mogadishu, Somalia—Black Hawk Down, In the Company of Heroes, and the Road to Unafraid. Streets of Mogadishu tells the rest of the tale—the untold stories of the real events of Task Force RANGER and those brave soldiers who truly gave their all.

Finally, I want to make specific mention of the book and movie

Black Hawk Down. I am personally very proud of both of them. I believe together they provide Americans with a better perspective of what took place there, versus the political perspective of a failed mission that was all wrong. Mark Bowden did a fantastic job of telling the story and I applaud his work. However, I must make it perfectly clear that I did not provide any input to Mark Bowden's book. I was on active duty in the Army until January 1, 2002; thus he knew that I would be unable to make any significant contribution. My first conversation with Mark occurred in September 2003 when I called him seeking help to locate some family members whose loved ones had died in Somalia. We had a pleasant conversation, but I did tell him my book would correct a few things that were incorrect in his book (about which we both laughed).

The movie's greatest asset is the fact that it was produced by Jerry Bruckheimer and directed by Ridley Scott, two of the best of the best. The actors were also great—Eric Bana, William Fichtner, Sam Shepard, Ewan McGregor, Jason Isaacs, Josh Hartnett, Orlando Bloom and Tom Sizemore, to name a few. Also, the movie had two excellent technical advisors: COL (Ret.) Tom Matthews and COL (Ret.) Lee Van Arsdale. Tom and Lee were members of Task Force RANGER in Mogadishu; Tom commanded the aviation assets of TF160th Special Operations Aviation Regiment, and Lee was a key figure in the Operations Center for Major General Garrison. These two professional soldiers of the Special Operations community were the perfect technical advisors.

I received four phone calls during the filming—two from Tom and Lee together and two from the actor Tom Sizemore, who portrayed me. I answered their respective questions in short conversations during these calls from Morocco. Although the movie was occasionally inconsistent with factual events in Somalia, it was very well done and told a great story that America deserved to know. My first opportunity to see the movie was on January 20, 2002 after its opening on January 18, just over two weeks after my first day of retirement from the Army. I thought the theater in Conyers, Georgia would be mostly empty since it was a 1:00 PM matinee on a Sunday, but it was packed. I watched the movie with some apprehension and numerous painful flashbacks. After the movie ended, I sat in place for a bit to compose myself before leaving the theater. When I started to leave I noticed there were still four or five people there. As I walked from my seat to the exit, I noticed a young couple still sitting there, but thought little of it. As I was passing their row, the young man glanced my way and we made eye contact. I stopped dead in my tracks as the young man walked my way. When he got to me, we gave each other a big hug and shed some tears. I had just watched the movie while sitting about two hundred feet from Ranger Sergeant Scott Galentine and his wife Casey. Scott had his thumb almost shot off in the streets of Mogadishu on October 3, 1993—this was properly depicted in the movie. Scott lived in Covington, Georgia, a short trip from where I lived in Snellville. There was a special reason Scott and I were there together in the theater that day in Conyers, Georgia—God knew we might need each other.

## Chain-of-Command

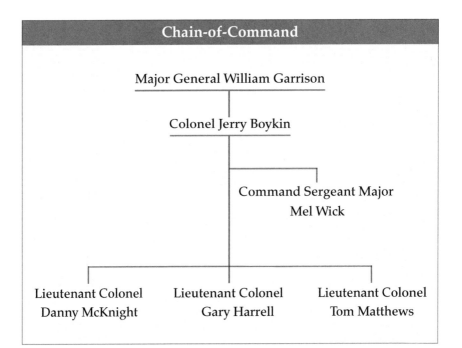

Major General William Garrison

Colonel Jerry Boykin

Command Sergeant Major Mel Wick

Lieutenant Colonel Danny McKnight

Lieutenant Colonel Gary Harrell

Lieutenant Colonel Tom Matthews

## Operational (Mission) Task Organization

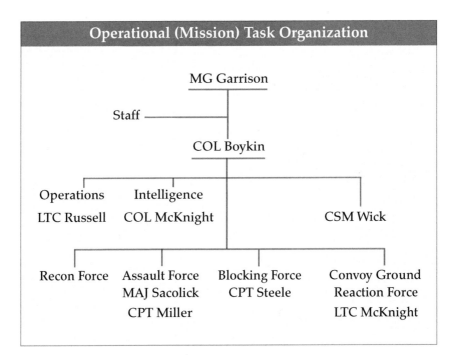

MG Garrison

Staff

COL Boykin

Operations LTC Russell

Intelligence COL McKnight

CSM Wick

Recon Force

Assault Force MAJ Sacolick CPT Miller

Blocking Force CPT Steele

Convoy Ground Reaction Force LTC McKnight

# The Dynamic Art of Leadership | 1

It was early in the battle on that fateful Sunday afternoon of October 3, 1993, in Mogadishu, Somalia, but I remember it like it was yesterday. The elements of Task Force RANGER had initiated the attack on the target building to capture two key members of warlord Mohamed Farah Aidid's leadership, exactly as planned. All air and ground insertion elements were in place, and the operation was progressing rapidly and smoothly. However, even the most successful operations can encounter difficulties that must be dealt with at some point—my first one surfaced about thirty minutes into the operation. While at the target building talking with a Delta Force operator about the loading of prisoners, I was informed that there was a critical casualty who needed to be evacuated immediately—Ranger Todd Blackburn.

Ranger Blackburn had fallen about forty-five feet while conducting the fast-rope insertion as part of the assault, and his injuries were serious. When I first saw him lying on the litter, he was bleeding profusely from the nose, mouth and ears. The medic, working on him feverishly, said he had internal injuries as well as back, neck and head injuries. He needed to be evacuated as soon as possible. It was time for my first tough decision as the senior leader/commander on the ground, so I made it. It was a tough one because the intensity of enemy fire had significantly increased everywhere, making the evacuation extremely difficult and very dangerous.

The decision itself is not the most important part of this process, but simply the *willingness* of a leader to act. Refusing to make a decision at all—whether good or bad—is to invite failure.

Now we'll see how one becomes a leader.

★   ★   ★   ★

Leadership is without a doubt the most dynamic art in existence today and one of the most important aspects, if not the most important, of the success of our great country. I believe that the American way of life, although not perfect, is the greatest in the world today. Why is it so successful? Because of our ideal of leadership that was formally established in July 1776 by brilliant leaders such as George Washington, Thomas Jefferson, John Adams, Benjamin Franklin and many others. These great leaders believed there was a better and more just way of life than that which existed under the tyrannical government of King George III of England. Thus, the Declaration of Independence was adopted on July 4, 1776 by the Continental Congress—a *hard right* decision made by great leaders. These men knew and understood that this pursuit of independence was not going to be easy, and it was not. However, they mutually pledged to each other their lives, their fortunes and their sacred honor. The pursuit of independence was extremely difficult but successful—the Treaty of Paris in 1783 ended the war and recognized the sovereignty of the United States. The personal courage exhibited by our Founding Fathers was intrinsic to the good leadership necessary for us to become the greatest nation in the world.

The art of leadership is so dynamic because of the interaction of many principles and concepts like values, commitment, professionalism, trust, responsibility, accountability, and decision-making. Leadership is actually an oxymoron of sorts in that it is simple but difficult. Leading is only easy on the days when everything goes as planned, but even those days require strength because things happen that make the plan irrelevant and ineffective; that is when good leadership is called upon to make decisions necessary to adjust and ensure success in the end. On the other hand, leading is fairly simple if we understand and effectively employ the principles and concepts of leadership. A very significant point to remember about leadership is this ... it does not matter if you are leading five people or five thousand people—leadership follows the same principles and concepts regardless.

It is also important to understand that the art of leadership, which is about people, is vastly different from the concept of management, which is about handling things like money, materials, transportation, food and schedules. The most precious and valuable resource in existence is that of people, and people deserve to be led, not managed. I know it is important to have good managers who manage things well, but to be truly successful as an organization, it is critically important to have good leaders. Furthermore, the best leaders are capable of leading people as well as managing things when necessary.

The values associated with leadership are those expressed by the Army abbreviation **L D R S H I P.**

| | |
|---|---|
| **Loyalty** | Bear true faith and allegiance to the U.S. Constitution, the Army, your unit, and other soldiers. |
| **Duty** | Fulfill your obligations. |
| **Respect** | Treat people as they should be treated. |
| **Selfless Service** | Put the welfare of the nation, the Army, and your subordinates before your own. |
| **Honor** | Live up to all the Army values. |
| **Integrity** | Do what's right, legally and morally. |
| **Personal Courage** | Face fear, danger, or adversity (physical or moral). |

These seven values are what I lived by in the Army for more than twenty-eight years. They are the cornerstones of Army service, both personally and professionally. The simplicity of leadership starts first and foremost with the understanding of these values and continues with the effective living of them. Now we see the beginning of leadership as a dynamic art. My ability as a leader was continuously developed throughout my 28-plus years in the Army because it was a way of life for me as a professional soldier/officer/leader, not just a job.

The significance of these seven values in leadership, however, is not unique to the Army; they are vital to everyday responsibilities like guiding your family and raising your children. I was raised in a home where my parents understood these values and instilled in their children loyalty, duty, respect, selfless service, honor, integrity, and personal courage. I can recall my father saying something like this to me, "Son, you told the people down the street you were going to have their lawn mowed by Friday. Well, today is Thursday; don't you think you should get it done?" I believe my father was simply pointing out that I had a duty to complete, which is the same thing I try to instill in my children and grandchildren.

★   ★   ★   ★

Now let's take a closer look at some of the seven values—those I label as high-powered leadership values. These are Personal Courage, Integrity, Honor, and Respect.

Personal courage is the willingness of a leader to make the *hard right* decision versus the *easy wrong* decision, which is so important because your right decision may not be looked upon favorably by all those you lead and may result in resistance by your subordinates. However, as a good leader with personal courage you must be steadfast in making the decision because it is beneficial to the organization. The benefits may be difficult to realize in the short term, but are definitely evident for the long term. The good leader is willing to make this kind of *hard right* decision because the number one focus is the success of the organization and the people, not their own popularity, personal interests or political correctness. Leadership is not a popularity contest and the personal courage you exhibit as a good leader is of utmost importance to the success of your organization and its people.

On the other hand, sometimes leaders are not willing to exhibit that personal courage and consequently make the *easy wrong* decision. Look at our great nation and think of examples where leaders were not willing to exhibit that necessary strength. Their own popularity, personal interests, and political correctness became more the focus than the interests of the organization and its people. This leader will say no to the *hard right* decision and choose the *easy wrong* so they can be liked and popular, thus leaving the *hard right* decision for someone else, which damages the organization and the people. When all is said and done, it comes down to this: give me a leader with the personal courage to make the *hard right* decision, and that leader I will follow anywhere, anytime.

If you want to find a leader who exhibited great personal courage in making a *hard right* decision versus an *easy wrong*, you need only look at the end of World War II. President Harry Truman's decision to bomb Hiroshima and Nagasaki was the ultimate *hard right* decision. It was clearly the right decision as it brought the war to an end and saved countless American lives. It was also an extremely hard decision to make because of the enormous number of Japanese civilians who would perish. The President listened to the advice of many subordinate leaders in making this decision; he heard all the pros and cons. However, in the end it was ultimately his responsibility; as he said "The buck stops here." The decision to bomb Japan has been much examined in the ensuing years, revealing both positive and negative aspects of the aftermath. The dissection of President Truman's decision clearly identifies that good leadership is not easy, and personal courage must override political correctness and popularity. It is a well-known fact that President Harry Truman had an abysmal approval rating, but I feel I want to thank him for leading our nation with his own personal courage.

A more recent President may be looked upon in much the same way as President Truman. He was not extremely popular but he led our country during the worst of times with great personal courage and the conviction to make the *hard right* decisions. Thank you, President George W. Bush, for staying committed to making our nation a safer place where my grandchildren can grow up and enjoy the American way of life.

Finally, understand that making the hard decision is far better than making the easy decision, and also far better than making no decision. If you are a no decision-making leader, then you are only allowing someone else to step in to fill the vacuum, and good leaders do not let that happen.

\* \* \* \*

The next high-powered leader value to be addressed is integrity, which is in a special category because of its overwhelming impact on people, especially leaders. It is something all of us have from the moment we arrive in this world; it makes you who you are as a person. It is a quality that nobody can ever take from you; you can only surrender it by negotiation and compromise.

Some people think that they can turn a profit by making a small compromise of integrity, but even this results in undermining who you really are as an individual. Furthermore, when you compromise once, it is generally easier to do so a second or third time, and before long your integrity is extinguished.

When considering the importance of integrity, I only need to look at my own military career. The first significant occasion where uncompromising, non-negotiable integrity was very evident to me was in 1980–81 when I was a Company Commander at Fort Benning, Georgia. As a young Captain, I was in command of C Company, 1st Battalion 58th Infantry, in the 197th Infantry Brigade; this level of command had approximately two hundred soldiers in the unit. I was fortunate to have in my first command opportunity some very experienced and exceptional non-commissioned officers, many of whom had served in combat in Vietnam. One such non-commissioned officer was SFC James Bondsteel, a Medal of Honor recipient for his actions on May 24, 1969, in the Republic of Vietnam. SFC Bondsteel, then an SSG, had earned his Medal of Honor about two weeks before I graduated high school in June 1969, and now here I was as his twenty-nine year old Company Commander.

SFC Bondsteel was one of my platoon sergeants—a superb leader and a tremendous trainer. I had actually heard a good bit about him prior to taking command of the company. My previous position at Fort Benning before being assigned to C Company, 1st Battalion 58th Infantry, was as the Aide-de-Camp to the Commanding General at Fort Benning, then Major General David E. Grange, Jr. I had been the General's Aide-de-Camp since September, 1978 when he commanded the 2nd Infantry Division in Korea. After completion of his command tour in Korea, then Major General Grange was assigned to Fort Benning in July, 1979 as the Commanding General, as well as the Commandant of the United States Army Infantry Center and Infantry School. I was assigned to Fort Benning as well, where I would continue as the Aide to Major General Grange until February, 1980.

I assumed command of C Company in March 1980, but not before receiving some clear, simple and to-the-point guidance from MG Grange regarding my Medal of Honor platoon sergeant, SFC James Bondsteel. He told me that SFC Bondsteel exceeded the Army weight standards and as a senior NCO and leader of soldiers that was unacceptable. MG Grange's integrity was such that this situation, even with a Medal of Honor recipient, was not something to be tolerated or overlooked. From a politically correct perspective, it would have been easy for the General to let the situation go because this man was a Medal of Honor recipient—do not disrespect or embarrass him. However, MG Grange was not willing to compromise his integrity and look the other way. He wanted SFC Bondsteel to lead by example, which in this instance meant meeting the Army weight standards just like the soldiers he was leading. MG Grange's uncompromising integrity was the focus of his guidance to me. He did not tell me what to do or how to get SFC Bondsteel to lose weight and meet the standards—he just told me to get it done. If SFC Bondsteel did not lose weight he could have been discharged from the Army for failure to comply with an Army standard—not a good thing for a living Medal of Honor recipient.

After a few weeks in command of the company, I had a lengthy session with SFC Bondsteel regarding the overweight issue. The idea of having to lose about thirty pounds was not a pleasant matter for him, but he understood why—he had to lead by example. Suffice to say this was not an easy process, but after numerous months of very specialized training, he finally achieved the Army weight standard. What a great lesson in never compromising your integrity, no matter how difficult the task.

\*   \*   \*   \*

Now let's look at the value of honor. My definition of honor is simply integrity multiplied because it should be associated with a profession, an organization, or an agency, not with an individual. Such association is based on the people in it, and the integrity of each individual is what makes it honorable.

I was privileged to serve in one of the most honorable professions in existence today—the United States Armed Forces, specifically the United States Army. As honorable a profession as it is, the Army has had to deal with dishonor in two very specific instances—one during the Vietnam War and one during the Iraq War.

The Vietnam incident that is so well known as dishonorable is the MyLai Massacre that occurred on March 16, 1968 in the small hamlet of MyLai in South Vietnam. The story of what happened there did not surface until November, 1969 when the platoon leader, Lieutenant William Calley, was implicated in the murders of more than one hundred villagers. After a lengthy military justice process, Lieutenant Calley was sentenced to life at hard labor on March 31, 1971—five months later on August 20th his sentence was reduced to twenty years. On September 2, 1972 the Army ended the inquiry into the MyLai Massacre with only a few others being punished. Even though there was overwhelming support for LT Calley from civilians, who objected to his being singled out for punishment, the dishonor brought on the U.S. Army was unprecedented and made the Vietnam War even more unpopular with the American people.

The second dishonorable incident occurred during the Iraq War. In early 2004 reports started surfacing of physical, psychological and sexual abuse of Iraqi prisoners in Abu Ghraib prison in 2003.

Investigation revealed that soldiers of the 320th Military Police Battalion had committed criminal acts of torture, homicide, rape and sodomy against Iraqi prisoners. There were eleven soldiers found guilty of some charges related to these despicable acts. Punishment ranged from no Discharges (2) to Bad Conduct Discharges (6) to Dishonorable Discharges (3), and prison sentences ranged from zero to ten years.

The most serious punishments were given to SPC Charles Graner (ten years in prison; Dishonorable Discharge), SSG Ivan Frederick (eight years in prison; Dishonorable Discharge), and SPC Lynndie England (three years in prison; Dishonorable Discharge). The most senior personnel directly affected by this incident were three officers: BG Janis Karpinski (Commander of all Iraq detention facilities), COL Thomas Pappas, and LTC Steven Jordan. BG Karpinski retired after a charge from a separate incident contributed to her demotion to Colonel. COL Pappas was relieved of his command and finished his career soon thereafter. Both Karpinski and Pappas were found guilty of dereliction of duty and reprimanded accordingly. LTC Jordan was acquitted of all charges related to prisoner mistreatment but received a reprimand for disobeying an order.

These reprehensible actions in Iraq by American soldiers of all ranks brought serious discredit and dishonor on the U.S. Army, its soldiers, and our Armed Forces in general. The failure of those soldiers to conduct themselves in an honorable manner was their downfall; they simply compromised their integrity. Many of those associated with this incident attempted to deflect the blame by saying that they had no detailed guidance regarding the treatment of the Iraqi prisoners, but the simple truth is that they all failed to demonstrate integrity.

The dishonor brought on the Army by these two incidents, separated by twenty-five years, was dealt with in a proper military manner. All the individuals in each case were properly handled through the military justice system and punished accordingly. A message was sent that rogue behavior like this would not be tolerated and that the honor of the military profession would not be tainted by the dishonorable actions of so few.

When considering the importance of honor it is critical to understand its importance outside of the military as well. The most prominent example of dishonor in our country's recent history outside of the military occurred in the White House on two occasions, 1974 and 1998. The 1974 event was associated with the Watergate break-in scandal in the summer of 1972 which was linked to those associated with the re-election campaign of President Richard Nixon. On August 8, 1974, President Nixon became the first President to resign in the history of our country. His resignation seems to be a true dichotomy, in my view, because it was both honorable and dishonorable. Honorable—in that President Nixon did the *hard right* thing and stepped down from the Presidency. Dishonorable—it was, and always will be, associated with an extremely shameful event.

Let's look at a more recent White House incident during the years of the Clinton Administration. In 1998, President Clinton was impeached by the House of Representatives on charges of perjury and obstruction of justice. He was subsequently acquitted of all charges after a 21-day Senate trial. The impeachment charges were brought against President Clinton because of allegations of sexual misconduct with Miss Monica Lewinsky. She alleged that nine sexual encounters had occurred between herself and President Clinton between November, 1995 and March, 1997. By the time news of this sexual relationship was made public on January 17, 1998, President Clinton was serving in his second term. On January 26, 1998, President Clinton spoke at a White House press conference where he stated, "I did not have sexual relations with that woman, Miss Lewinsky." The evidence regarding their sexual relations seemed to be quite significant to the American public, but the subsequent acquittal on all impeachment charges made it all go away—sort of. The vast majority of American citizens still believed something sexual had occurred. To this day, it is very clear that President Clinton's sexual misconduct brought an enormous amount of discredit and dishonor on the Office of the President of the United States, and specifically on Bill Clinton when he chose to put himself above the Office of the President. Personally, I felt that as an American soldier my Commander-in-Chief had done a dishonorable thing and was not honorable enough to tell the truth. A rank-in-file soldier in a similar situation with such compelling evidence would have faced serious consequences. The Commander-in-Chief had set a terrible example for young soldiers and young Americans in general. As it is said, actions speak louder than words.

The men and women who serve our country daily, whether in peace or war, are to me the ultimate example of honor. It is simply stated "greater love hath no one than this, that they lay down their life for another." The men and women of our military have been living that truth for many, many years.

There are innumerable examples of honor associated with the military profession. For example, if you were to read the citations for the Medal of Honor recipients in the history of our military, you would find that each and everyone was based on sacrifice, the honor associated with serving our country, and never letting a fellow comrade down, regardless of the consequences. I know this first hand because it was my great privilege to serve with four Medal of Honor recipients and meet several others.

One of those whom I met was George E. "Bud" Day, Colonel, United States Air Force (Retired). On August 26, 1967, Major Day was shot down over North Vietnam. He was immediately captured and taken to an underground camp where he was questioned, then tortured for refusing to answer questions. On the fifth day in this camp, he managed to escape even though he was badly injured. After about fifteen days of evading the enemy, Bud Day was re-captured by the North Vietnamese and taken back to the same underground camp he had escaped from earlier. He had been shot twice when re-captured by the North Vietnamese soldiers, but nevertheless, was immediately tortured upon his return to the camp. After a few days there, Bud Day was moved to the infamous "Hanoi Hilton" where he would remain for almost six years as a POW until his release on March 14, 1973. He was continually tortured but maintained his resistance and never gave in. While at the "Hanoi Hilton," his wounds remained untreated and became infected. He suffered from malnutrition, as did most POWs. He also continued to be brutally tortured which caused serious problems to his hands, fingers and body as a whole. On one occasion in 1971, guards burst in on some of the American POWs as they were gathered for a religious service that was forbidden by the North Vietnamese. With rifles in their faces, Major Bud Day stood up, looked directly at the North Vietnamese and their rifles, then proceeded to sing "The Star Spangled Banner." He was joined by the other prisoners, including the ranking U.S. POW, then-Navy Captain James Stockdale, another

Medal of Honor recipient. Colonel Bud Day is the epitome of the sacrifice and honor that is at the core of those serving in the United States Armed Forces—Army, Air Force, Navy, Marines, and Coast Guard. As a footnote to this testament of true honor, Senator John McCain has clearly stated that he owes his life to Bud Day and Norris Overly from their time in the Hanoi Hilton.

Thus, each one of us individually makes our profession, organization, or agency honorable, and it is our responsibility to maintain that honor through our integrity. My perspective is significantly impacted by my time with Task Force RANGER in Somalia and my service with heroes like Tom Ditomasso, Jeff Struecker, Casey Joyce, Dominick Pilla, Jamie Smith, Karl Maier, and of course, Medal of Honor recipients Gary Gordon and Randy Shughart. These men and many others like them were the personification of honor.

*  *  *  *

The last of these high-powered leader values is respect, which is my most important of all. This realization came to me in July 2003, when I was speaking at Fort Knox, Kentucky as part of a leadership training program for Army ROTC cadets, most of whom would eventually be commissioned as officers in the United States Army. During the question and answer session a cadet asked me, "Sir, of the seven values of LDRSHIP, which one do you think is most important?" After a momentary pause, my response, "Respect."

There are various levels of respect associated with leadership, the most essential of which is the respect that subordinates have for their leader. Why are subordinates respectful? Is it because they feel they have to be, or because they really want to be? If leaders are re-spected simply because they are in the top position, or make the most money, or happen to be the most senior persons, these are all the wrong reasons. Unfortunately this occurs all too often.

The next level of respect in leadership is the mutual respect that should exist amongst peers. This is very important because every day is not a good day. For instance, as a Battalion Commander in the Army on two occasions I was privileged to lead and command units of approximately eight hundred fifty soldiers—an Infantry Battalion at Schofield Barracks, Hawaii, and a Ranger Battalion at Fort Benning, Georgia. While commanding those battalions, I had a few bad days because the American soldier can create some of the most amazing problems that you could ever imagine in your life. Generally I could handle them, but there were a few times I needed some help. The last place I wanted to go for help was my boss be-cause he expected me to be solving the problems, which is why I was there as the commander of the unit. So I always turned to my peers for help, which further solidified the trust and respect we had for each other.

The last, and most crucial, level of respect is that which a leader must have for subordinates. As leaders, we must respect those whom we are privileged to lead every day. Regrettably some leaders, usu-ally the bad ones, never seem to understand this. After all, they only exist because of the dedication and service of their subordinates; therefore, respecting them for what they do and how they do it is key to successful leadership. It is also the only way in which a leader can *earn* respect; subordinates who know they receive it will go to the earth's end to accomplish a mission, no matter how difficult and challenging.

\* \* \* \*

To see these high-power aspects of leadership in action, we need only look at an incident during the Vietnam War. On November 14, 1965 one of the most significant battles of the Vietnam War took place in the Central Highlands of South Vietnam. On this day, approximately four hundred fifty soldiers of the 1st Battalion, 7th Cavalry, under the command of then—Lieutenant Colonel Hal Moore, were dropped into the Ia Drang Valley at Landing Zone X-Ray via sixteen UH-1 helicopters, or Hueys. The battle that ensued lasted over three days and two nights and was chronicled in the book, *We Were Soldiers Once ... And Young* by LTG (Ret.) Harold G. Moore and Joseph L. Galloway, the United Press International reporter at LZ X-Ray. Ten years after the book's release, the movie *We Were Soldiers* was released on the big screen for all of America to see the heroic story of honor, commitment, courage, and sacrifice that took place those November days of 1965 in the Ia Drang Valley. The aftermath of what occurred in those three days of raging battle at LZ X-Ray had a profound impact on the Vietnam War. The tragic results in terms of people killed and wounded on both sides were as follows: seventy-nine Americans killed in action, one hundred twenty-one wounded in action, and none missing; there were also approximately six hundred fifty enemy dead in direct combat, with an estimated twelve hundred fifteen killed and wounded by artillery, air attacks, and aerial rockets, and six enemy prisoners captured and evacuated. Those four hundred fifty American soldiers had battled over two thousand enemy soldiers for days and did so because of the values that had been deeply ingrained in them, and the leaders at all levels led by example throughout the battle.

Soon after taking command of 3rd Ranger Battalion in February 1993, I was able to schedule a very significant professional development training session for my officers and non-commissioned officers—that is, the ranks of Corporal to Sergeant Major. Combining officers and NCOs in the same professional development session was rare almost to the point of being unheard of, but on April 2, 1993, both groups of soldiers were privileged to hear about the reality of combat that took place at LZ X-Ray from LTG Hal Moore and Mr. Joe Galloway. Leadership, respect, commitment, courage, honor, and willingness to sacrifice for your fellow comrades have never been spoken about any better than on that April day in 1993 by these two great men. Of all the things that came across loud and clear from LTG Moore was the awesome respect he had for his soldiers. He and his Command Sergeant Major Basil Plumley made it perfectly clear to their soldiers of 1st Bn, 7th Cav that whatever was to be done would be done by everyone from the lowest ranking soldier right up to and including the Command Sergeant Major and the Battalion Commander.

LTG Moore believed in the simple philosophy of being able to do everything your soldiers could do and doing it with them. He exhibited some of the greatest leadership in the history of combat in our military. He led from the front and led by example. He was literally the first to step off the helicopter onto the ground at LZ X-Ray on November 14, 1965 and on November 16 he was the last to step off the ground. That was the promise he made to his soldiers—no one would put himself in any danger that LTG Moore himself would not do—and he kept that promise at great risk to his life.

That is great leadership.

Although I had always hoped I could lead in combat as well as this man, I certainly never thought I would be confronted with such a harrowing combat situation. But I was wrong. The lessons we learned from LTG Moore and Joe Galloway were invaluable during the battle on October 3–4, 1993 in Mogadishu, Somalia. We faced similar odds and fought for all the same reasons. Thank you, LTG (Ret.) Hal Moore, for preparing us to confront the kind of overwhelming odds seldom seen in war.

I was able to improve my own skill in leadership by learning from both good and bad leaders, but when I look back at my military journey of twenty-eight-plus years, I see primarily the influence of great leadership. The names that immediately come to mind are Lieutenant General (Retired) David E. Grange, Jr. (father), General (Retired) William F. Kernan, Brigadier General (Retired) David L. Grange (son), Lieutenant General (Retired) William G. Boykin, and Command Sergeant Major (Retired) Marianno Leon-Guerrero. These five special leaders shaped my growth more than anybody, and probably more than they even realize. Their impact was so significant because there were certain constants that permeated all of their leadership styles—leading by example, being honest and forthright with those you lead, doing the right thing, exhibiting personal courage in your decision-making, and respecting the subordinates you are privileged to lead.

I would be remiss, however, if I did not acknowledge a few other great mentors, including Tom Fincher, Joe Stringham, Wes Taylor, Frank Akers, William Garrison, George Fisher and Charles Cady, all of whom are retired senior leaders in the U.S. Army, and who made it perfectly clear to me that leading was not easy, but an awesome privilege in life.

I also had the unique privilege to work for a father and his son.

As previously stated, I was the Aide-de-Camp for LTG (Ret.) David E. Grange, Jr., and was the 3rd Ranger Battalion Commander when his son, BG (Ret.) David L. Grange was the Commander of the 75th Ranger Regiment. Yes, I was truly blessed in my career.

Let me elaborate just a little about LTG (Ret.) Grange's career and our relationship. As his Aide-de-Camp in Korea while he was the Division Commander of the 2nd Infantry Division at Camp Casey, I saw then MG Grange do twelve-mile road marches with soldiers in the various divisional units. This periodic training was required for all divisional soldiers, which included the two of us. But to meet the requirement he always wanted to do the training with the soldiers. He and I probably did at least one road march every other month, whereas the requirement for all soldiers was only quarterly.

I also had the unique opportunity to participate in a DMZ patrol[1] operation between South and North Korea in 1979 with MG Grange. The Division Commander and I walked a patrol late one night with the unit on the DMZ border security mission at the time. Once again, there he was doing what his soldiers had to do and doing it with them.

How blessed I was to learn so much from this great man/leader. He had begun his military career as a teenage enlisted soldier in WWII, and then became an officer through Officer Candidate School. He was a Captain Company Commander in the Korean War and participated in a combat airborne parachute assault during that war. He was a Brigade Commander in the 101st Airborne Division during the Vietnam War while his son Lieutenant David L. Grange was in combat in Vietnam at the same time. LTG (Ret.) David E. Grange, Jr. is truly a legend in the U.S. Army. The annual event known as Best Ranger Competition[2] at Fort Benning, Georgia, is named after him. Personally, it was an honor and privilege to be his Aide- de-Camp for almost eighteen months (Korea and Ft. Benning). He taught me to lead not just by words but by actions. He also made me a better leader, a better commander, and a better person than I would have otherwise been, just as the other great leaders did whom I have mentioned.

I also worked for just a few bad leaders—names withheld—but their impact was also important because they identified things I did not want to do. Fortunately, bad leadership is much less prevalent than good. It is also easy to recognize. For instance, an Army commander I once knew used to visit training only when the weather conditions were sixty–eighty degrees and sunny. This same commander would never be found visiting training when it was thirty degrees and raining. Those whom you are leading need you a lot more on the thirty-degree days than on the sixty-degree days. Generally leaders of this sort are more interested in their own success than that of their subordinates and the organization, and they never reach the point of respecting their subordinates above all else.

# The Making of a Leader | 2

We have all heard people say someone was "born to be a leader," as if someone can be born with some innate ability that automatically makes them a leader, but this is false. Leaders can only be *made*. Once their ability is developed by hard experience and devotion to the principles of LDRSHIP, the next important part is simply the matter of opportunity. Many people develop the ability to lead but never get a formal opportunity to exercise that responsibility. On the other hand, many people who believe that they are equipped with the ability to lead are given such an opportunity but unfortunately are not up to the challenge, and thus we have a bad leader—and a dangerous situation.

Since the beginning of the twenty-first century, there have been two devastating incidents in our country's history that depict American leadership at its best—and at its worst. The first incident is the horrific tragedy of September 11, 2001, when our great nation was attacked by terrorists. Many leaders stepped forward and had a powerful impact on that day and the days and months and years that followed, but no one was more steadfast than Mayor Rudy Giuliani of New York City. On that day, and during the recovery, the world saw a leader who led by example, assumed responsibility and accountability for actions to be taken, and had the personal courage to make *hard right* decisions. I will always remember the picture of him walking down the streets of Manhattan with a law enforcement officer on one side and a fire-rescue officer on the other—leading, like LTG Hal Moore, by example.

Conversely a bad leader exhibits little or no personal courage in making *hard right* decisions, does not truly assume the responsibility and accountability for actions that should occur, and certainly does not lead by example. Look only to catastrophic events associated with the natural disaster of Hurricane Katrina. There were numerous people who failed miserably in their leadership during this terrible time, but none did worse than the Mayor of New Orleans. Very simply, Mayor Ray Nagin failed to lead. He did not make the *hard right* decisions, but instead the *easy wrong* decisions.

First *of these* was allowing people to decide whether to evacuate the area. People will never want to leave their homes regardless of the danger involved with staying; growing up in Florida where hurricanes have posed a danger on many occasions made this very clear to me. In the case of Hurricane Katrina, the enormous danger of letting people remain in their homes was clearly evident. The impact of this *easy wrong* decision was unfortunately realized when Hurricane Katrina hit New Orleans with relentless and unforgiving force. The aftermath of this situation yielded nearly incalculable damage to property and hundreds of fatalities—a tragedy that might have been averted, or ameliorated, if Mayor Nagin had the personal courage to make the *hard right* decision in spite of the legal prohibitions against ordering citizens to leave their homes.

The Mayor also shirked responsibility and condemned the actions, or inaction, of those leaders above him. He wanted to point the finger at the Governor of Louisiana, the Director of the Federal Emergency Management Agency (FEMA), and even the President of the United States. True, there may have been some blame to be shared, but the mayor himself was responsible for the bad leadership in New Orleans during that time.

\*    \*    \*    \*

Now let me share some thoughts on my personal development as a leader. It started very early because of my family and my community, two aspects of life that have a profound impact on all of us and are most likely to help determine any success we may achieve.

First, my family … I was blessed to have a father, mother, and two brothers who were a positive force in my life. My father was a man who led others by actions, not by words. He was my Little League baseball coach, which was good for me because it allowed me to learn about things like integrity, respect, duty, discipline, hard work, responsibility, and commitment. But it was also challenging because the player my father was always the toughest on was me.

My father was a leader in everything he did, not just as a Little League coach; he was a leader in his profession, as a laboratory and X-ray technician in a medical clinic, and in the Church, serving as a deacon for many years. He was also a highly respected man in our community of Rockledge, Florida. All in all, my father was the greatest man and best leader I have known in my life.

My mother had a very special influence on her three boys (four, counting my dad). She had the toughest job of anyone as a stay-at-home mom. While my father was at work for ten or twelve hours a day, five or six days a week, my mother was at home making sure everything was right. There were many times that my mother had to shoulder the responsibility for the discipline and guidance of her boys, and she was as great a leader as my father.

I was a middle child—Bill was four years older and Jim was five years younger—and both helped me develop as a person and a leader.

Bill was a positive influence because I was able to watch him grow up and develop as a leader himself—he was a high school quarterback, and later a terrific athletic director and football coach in the public school system. Because of my high school baseball experiences and the leadership lessons I had learned I was able to help Jim by guiding and encouraging him to work hard all the time. I feel proud to have helped lead him to become an exceptional baseball player in high school, college and almost the pros had it not been for an untimely injury. Jim continues to be an outstanding professional leader in our hometown of Rockledge, Florida, serving for over twenty-five years as its city manager.

I was also blessed to grow up in a fabulous community that was unique and special in the 1960s—and still is today. It was relatively small, but vibrant with activity. I grew up in Cocoa-Rockledge, Florida, which is located on Central Florida's east coast in Brevard County. The community was filled with wonderful activities and opportunities because the most significant Space Center on earth is located there—originally called the Cape Canaveral Air Force Station, it's now known as Kennedy Space Center. I remember watching missile launches from the front yard, like the one with our first astronaut, an American hero named Alan Shepard. These were amazing times for our country but even more amazing for those of us who lived there.

This was also a community of close-knit families. We all attended the same high school since there was only one in Cocoa-Rockledge in those days, fortunately a very good one both academically and athletically. I was fortunate to be in numerous academic and athletic leadership positions during my junior high and high school years. Probably the most significant was in my senior year of high school when I was the quarterback on our football team. Since the team was 0–10 the year before this was difficult, and definitely challenging, but I believe it turned out to be one of the most important aspects in my development as a leader.

One specific example: after starting the season in October 1968 with two close losses, we faced a highly ranked Titusville High team on its home field with more than five thousand spectators in the stadium. We were outsized, outmanned and outgunned, and in a totally hostile environment—not the recipe for getting the first win of the season. The game did not start well for us; it was 14-0 in their favor at the end of the first quarter, but we did not give up or back down, we just played harder. At halftime they were leading, but only 20–13. In the second half, the score went back and forth… from a 20–20 tie to them leading 26–20, to us leading 27–26, to them leading 33–27, then to us finally winning 34–33. The winning point was scored when I scrambled and dove into the end zone, just crossing the goal line. It was without question the best game in my quarterbacking career, and the local newspaper wrote "the little general who ambushed Titusville showed poise beyond his years and experience." And one of my coaches, Dick Blake, who later became the principal of our high school, said, "In terms of mental and physical toughness and leadership skills, Danny McKnight had the admiration of the faculty, students, and athletes."

And it just so happened that this football game was played on October 4, 1968, exactly twenty-five years before the events of Somalia known as "Black Hawk Down."

*　*　*　*

After graduating from high school in 1969, a very important part of my leadership development was to continue my education. I stayed at home to attend Brevard Junior College, now Brevard Community College, for two years before moving to Tallahassee, Florida where I attended Florida State University. There I earned two degrees, a Bachelor of Science in Business Management and a "professional" military degree through Army ROTC—this was not a formal degree, but what I call the beginning of my "professional" degree in the U.S. Army.

On August 3, 1973, I was commissioned as an officer in the United States Army. As with everything I did in my life, I wanted to be the best I could possibly be, which meant that I had to be in the middle of the action. To me, this meant being an infantry officer and, eventually, being an Airborne Ranger. After my commissioning as an Infantry 2nd Lieutenant on that August day, I reported to Fort Benning, Georgia to attend the Infantry Officer Basic Course—the journey was now underway. After graduation, I entered Airborne School in December 1973 and received my airborne jump wings.

In January 1974, I entered Ranger School and began the toughest leadership course in the United States Army. It was the toughest challenge of my life up to that point—a fifty-eight-day course that pushed you to the limits physically, mentally, and emotionally. My goal was not just to graduate from the course and be Ranger-qualified, but to graduate as the Distinguished Honor Graduate (#1 in the class). This was a self-imposed challenge that was even more difficult than usual because mine was a winter class. That meant that we would endure harsh and adverse conditions between January and March, 1974—particularly hard on someone who grew up in Florida and had never even seen snow.

The cold weather challenge was very significant for me, both physically and mentally. It taught me how important it is to overcome things you have never encountered. The physical aspects of cold weather are tough enough to deal with, but in my opinion, the mental parts are even tougher, especially when you are the leader. As a Ranger Student in Dahlonega, Georgia in February 1974, I was in a leadership position in some extremely cold weather and snow. As a leader you must set the example, for those you are leading look to you. Let it suffice to say that as a Ranger Student I learned so much about leading regardless of how tired, how hungry, or how hot or cold you might be—a lesson that would stay with me for the next twenty-eight years.

Despite my best efforts, I did not reach my desired goal of being the Distinguished Honor Graduate, but I did achieve being an Honor Graduate—and number two in the class. Only two weeks after graduating from Ranger School, I reported to my first duty location in Dahlonega, Georgia, where I was assigned for the next three years as a Ranger Instructor in the Mountain Phase of Ranger

School (including the coldest part of the Ranger Course). During this three-year assignment, I learned leadership skills from some of the best officers and non-commissioned officers our Army had in the 1960s and 1970s—my career was off to a special and blessed beginning.

# The Privilege of Leading  |  3

During my amazing journey in the Army, I was privileged to command and lead soldiers as a Company Commander (Captain) in 1980-81, and as a Battalion Commander (Lieutenant Colonel) on two occasions. My first opportunity to command at the battalion level was in the 25th Infantry Division where I commanded from June 1991 to January 1993. My second was at Fort Benning, Georgia, where I commanded 3rd Battalion, 75th Ranger Regiment from February 1993 to July 1994. My time as a Company and Battalion Commander was awesome and filled with fantastic training events in places such as Alaska (1980), Australia (1992) and Korea (1993). Most important, however, is the fact that I was privileged to lead the greatest soldiers in the world, those of our United States Army.

My first opportunity to command was at Fort Benning where I commanded a mechanized infantry company (Charlie Company) in the 1st Battalion, 58th Infantry. One of the best experiences during this twenty-two month command occurred in December 1980.

My Company had been selected to participate in training at the Northern Warfare Training Center in Fort Greely, Alaska—the ultimate cold weather training challenge. The unit of about one hundred eighty-five soldiers, which included my Company plus some routine attached elements of fire support personnel, engineer personnel, and medical personnel, deployed from Fort Benning on December 1, 1980. I was thrilled about this first major deployment as a Company Commander, but also understood the tremendous responsibility associated with this extreme cold weather training event. The training plan was simple—train for three weeks in an extreme cold weather environment to learn how to execute basic soldier and unit tasks. The unit landed on Allen Army Airfield at Fort Greely late on December 1st; the temperature was minus 29 degrees, which was nearly one hundred degrees colder than Fort Benning. Even more astonishing was the fact that 29-below was going to be the high temperature for the next three weeks at Fort Greely.

The first few days included an orientation and the issuing of cold weather clothing and equipment followed by classroom instruction on equipment handling and ski/snowshoe training. Late in the first week a major snowfall of about four feet blanketed the training area. The living conditions varied from small buildings with bunks/bathrooms/heat (first week) to large tents with sleeping bags/heating stoves/outside wooden port-a-johns (second week) to the final week of a three-day exercise in the field with small tents/sleeping bags. This three-day exercise was composed of sixteen-to-eighteen hour training days that included ski/snowshoe movements, weapons firing, and small unit tactics. The temperatures ranged from minus-50 to minus-55, an environment in which it was difficult not just to train but to survive. The unit would depart and return to Fort Benning on December 22nd, but only after completing its final task of loading the unit's equipment on the aircraft in the brutally bitter cold, which with wind chill, fell to minus-94 degrees. This equipment loading process was very slow because soldiers had to rotate every ten minutes to avoid serious frostbite. During this training period, there had been some cold weather injuries, mainly minor frostbite, but no loss of fingers or toes.

Everyone was ecstatic to return to Fort Benning and its much warmer temperatures. Each and every soldier learned a great deal about the challenges of cold weather training while learning even more about themselves. Personally, the cold weather environment taught me a lot about the soldiers and the training challenges. However, most important, the arduous conditions during that three-week training event further developed me as a leader and made clear the importance of training with your soldiers and leading by example.

The next command opportunity for me came along in 1991 when I was selected to be a Battalion Commander; my command was the 4th Battalion, 27th Infantry (Wolfhounds). For a Florida boy, it was absolutely the perfect place to command—Schofield Barracks, Hawaii on the island of Oahu. In addition, I was blessed to lead a light infantry battalion in one of the Army's finest divisions, the 25th Infantry Division.

Although there were numerous highlights and challenges during this command, one stood out from them all. The Battalion was selected as the Division's Infantry Battalion to participate in the Kangaroo 92 Exercise—an every-other-year training exercise that takes place in Australia with its military. My Battalion would actually become a Battalion Task Force, as it would be augmented with other go-to-war elements of field artillery, air defense artillery, engineers, combat support and aviation (7 UH-60 Black Hawk helicopters and 3 CH-47 Chinook helicopters). The Battalion Task Force (BnTF) would total approximately one thousand soldiers.

In preparation for the deployment and the exercise, my primary staff personnel and I made two coordination visits to Australia. The exercise itself would last about two weeks; however, the BnTF would deploy earlier in order to conduct unit training, as well as make final preparations for the exercise. The BnTF deployed from Hickham Air Force Base in Honolulu on March 1, 1992. After a flight of almost eleven hours with a refueling stop in Guam, the BnTF landed in Darwin, Australia. We then moved directly to our field location in the northern territory commonly referred to as the Outback. The field location became our home—numerous large tents, cots for sleeping, no running water, and a small number of vehicles.

The terrain there was rough and the weather was hot and humid with occasional violent thunderstorms. The temperature would reach 105 degrees with ninety percent humidity almost every day; the fierce thunderstorms were an experience alone—the lightning was extraordinary, and the rain was simply torrential. These weather conditions usually limited training intensity from two to four pm.

The BnTF conducted their training separately from any Aussie units for the first couple of weeks. These day-and-night training events included platoon level evaluations, company-platoon live fire exercises and air assault operations. The training opportunities were fantastic and very challenging; the leaders at all levels did a superb job of maximizing the training for the soldiers. As a matter of routine, I participated in the training at all levels from squad to platoon to company. I even conducted a few platoon evaluations;

yes, a few platoon leaders (Lieutenants), platoon sergeants (Sergeants First Class), and forty other soldiers were so "lucky" as to have the Battalion Commander as their evaluator. This would surprise some leaders because it might seem to be a level too low in the chain of command for the BN Cdr to evaluate, but I believe it was the perfect way for me to assess the training effectiveness of both the platoon and the company leadership. It also gave me the opportunity to train with the soldiers. Furthermore, in these challenging training conditions of tough weather and terrain, I was able to determine better the unique strengths and weaknesses of the units.

After the rigorous BnTF training period ended, the Kangaroo 92 Exercise began and lasted about ten days. This was exceptional training as well, especially with forces from another superb Army like the Australians. The experience was terrific for every soldier in the BnTF, but most especially for the leaders. Without question, the performance of the BnTF was nothing less than outstanding, as stated by the Australian General we worked for during the exercise.

The final phase of the BnTF deployment would consist of R&R (Rest & Relaxation) in the city of Darwin; the BnTF was divided into three equal groupings for a separate one-and-a-half day R&R visit to Darwin. The soldiers enjoyed their time off and the interaction with the Aussie people. The last group's R&R time was cut a little short because a typhoon was rapidly approaching Australia and would impact the area of Darwin, which it did, with winds of over a hundred miles per hour, but not before we had everyone back from R&R and relocated to a gymnasium. On April 10, 1992 the BnTF redeployed to Hawaii, exhausted but much improved by one of the finest leading/training opportunities in my career. Every member of the BnTF was better trained in some way at its conclusion.

When I assumed command of 3rd Ranger Battalion at Fort Benning on February 11, 1993, it was one of the most special moments in my life. In January, I had just completed eighteen months of battalion command in Hawaii, and now I was blessed to be a Ranger Battalion Commander. When I stood in front of eight hundred fifty-plus Rangers on Peden Field at Fort Benning that February day in 1993, it was easy to know what to say, as well as what not to say. As the incoming Commander, you normally say very little because most of the speaking time is taken by the outgoing Commander to say thank you and farewell to everyone. I had served in this Ranger Battalion previously when I was the Battalion Executive Officer from July 1989 to May 1990. In December 1989 I went to combat with 3rd Battalion as part of Operation JUST CAUSE in Panama; many of those standing on Peden Field the day I assumed command were there as well.

This combat operation was the first for the 75th Ranger Regiment since its reorganization in October 1984 when 3rd Ranger Battalion joined 1st and 2nd Ranger Battalions. The alert for this operation occurred on December 19, which was about five days after rehearsals for a possible mission in Panama that was completed by various Special Operations Forces. As the Battalion Executive Officer, I was in charge of the second command and control element for 3rd Battalion when we executed the combat airborne assault at Rio Hato Airfield in conjunction with 2nd Ranger Battalion. This airborne assault was executed under enemy fire—enemy bullets were piercing the aircrafts during the jump. On some aircrafts there were Rangers wounded before they ever exited the plane, thus unable to get on the ground. This airborne assault occurred at 1:03 am on December 21st from an altitude of five hundred feet, an altitude used for combat jumps only (as compared to routine training jumps, which are normally made at 1200 feet). This shorter time in the air under the parachute was a good thing because the bullets, easily detected by the tracer rounds flaring in the darkness, were flying by on the way down.

The airborne assault was very successful and we seized control of the Rio Hato Airfield while confiscating many weapons and capturing numerous enemy soldiers. The 7th Infantry Division would arrive at Rio Hato Airfield a few days later and take control of it from us. This relief in place operation freed the Ranger Battalions from Rio Hato, which allowed them to conduct numerous other follow-on missions on key targets over the next ten to twelve days.

This was my initial experience in combat, but not my last. As the second in command of 3rd Ranger Battalion, it was an especially amazing experience and a special privilege; the simple fact of leading Rangers in combat is beyond explanation. However, in combat operations like JUST CAUSE there is the ever-present risk of losing fellow Rangers in battle. We had two KIAs that first day—the pain of that sacrifice is never easy. Nevertheless in the end there was a great feeling of pride about the mission's success with minimal casualties. I must say that fighting alongside the best of the best, the Army Rangers and other Special Operations Forces, is extraordinary and always will be so.

From my previous time in the Ranger Regiment, I knew many of those standing on the field that day, and many knew me, but that was history to them, and what really mattered was that I was their Battalion Commander. The most important thing I did say to the Rangers of 3rd Ranger Battalion was, " I want you to understand something very simple: from this moment until the day I give up command of this great Battalion, I will never ask you to do anything that I cannot do and will not do with you." I wanted all the Rangers to know that the most important thing was what they did and how they did it, and that was *every day*. This was especially important because I was commanding/leading a special operations unit that could be deployed to combat on short notice anywhere in the world at any time; and almost every time they would be at the tip of the spear.

This was a bold statement because I knew the challenges associated with these words were many. It is critically important that a leader be honest with those they are privileged to lead, so if you say something, as I did that day, you had better be able to meet all future challenges successfully. It is a very simple fact that as a leader you better be able to do what you say to your subordinates because if you cannot, they will "eat your lunch," and you will lose them forever. I knew the challenges were coming my way because those eight hundred fifty Ranger studs were questioning how the Battalion Commander (soon to be forty-two years old) could possibly do what they could do. And believe this: they were physically and mentally and emotionally tough, but I had a plan about how I would successfully meet the forthcoming challenges, and ultimately earn their respect.

*    *    *    *

My plan was fairly simple in that it focused on basic routine things, not just special events, but as it turned out, the first opportunity presented to me as the new 3rd Ranger Battalion Commander was a significantly special event—a major deployment for the battalion to the Republic of South Korea as part of an exercise called Team Spirit.

Upon taking command in February 1993, I was immediately immersed in the final stages of preparation for this deployment less than one month later, on March 1, 1993. The plan required the battalion to fly from Fort Benning, Georgia, to McChord Air Force Base in Seattle, Washington, where we would have a brief layover to change to other aircraft that would fly us non-stop to South Korea. This last leg of the trip would require the aircraft to execute an in-flight air-refueling operation, as well as require the Rangers to conduct an in-flight rigging for the battalion's mass tactical airborne assault operation into Pohang, South Korea. This battalion airborne insertion was a very big deal because there had not been any such airborne operation in South Korea since the Korean War.

Our airborne insertion into the Pohang Drop Zone was part of the battalion's initial mission in the Team Spirit Exercise. The airborne operation was very successful, with no major injuries, only a few minor ones, and a few uncomfortable Rangers who landed in cold wet rice paddies. The late afternoon temperature when we executed the jump was about 40 degrees and wet—a bad combination.

This undertaking was not the end of the battalion's initial mission, just the beginning; the end would actually occur approximately forty hours later. After completion of the tactical assembly of the battalion on the drop zone, which essentially entailed accountability of all personnel and equipment prior to proceeding with the next phase of the mission, we prepared for movement, and then started moving toward the initial mission objective area.

The first day/night movement involved crossing streams and creeks, as well as traversing mountains. After midnight, we did stop in a patrol base for about four hours in order to sleep (about two hours sleep per Ranger as some were always on guard for security reasons), conduct equipment maintenance (like cleaning weapons), conduct personal hygiene (brush teeth, change socks), eat something simple, and prepare for the next twenty-four hours. The temperatures that night and morning were in the mid-20s.

The second day/night movement was very arduous; the mountain crossings became even more challenging and the terrain more difficult as we closed in on the mission objective area. There was only a brief halt during this movement, around midnight, expressly for the final preparation of execution of the mission (attacking the opposing forces position). As planned, we attacked the enemy position during the early morning hours when it was cold and still dark. The attack was overwhelmingly successful—mission accomplished. The Rangers of 3rd Battalion had performed superbly, so much so that the United States Marine Corps Major General under whom we were operating said, "You Rangers are the damndest thing I have ever seen … fly all the way from Fort Benning to South Korea, execute a flawless airborne insertion, then move for almost two days before attacking and destroying the enemy; that is an amazing performance." The Rangers earned this great compliment, but more important earned the respect of the USMC 2-star General.

After about three weeks and the completion of all our missions in the Team Spirit Exercise, we redeployed back home to Fort Benning. As I looked back on that awesome experience and special opportunity, I realized something very significant had taken place that was not even planned: it had been a test for the new Battalion Commander—me. I was observed closely and evaluated by eight hundred-plus Rangers from start to finish, who witnessed first hand that a Battalion Commander could and would do everything that the Rangers were doing—carry a ruck, cross the streams, climb the mountains, endure the cold. All of this I did with them. I am certain that if I hadn't, I would have lost my hold over those Rangers as their leader. So this special training event provided me the opportunity for a great start to commanding 3rd Ranger Battalion.

★　★　★　★

I continued to be successful as a leader because I adhered to the principle that basic routine things matter the most to your subordinates, not some rare special event. The two things on which I concentrated from the beginning were very simple but extremely important aspects of soldiering in a Ranger Battalion—total fitness and training. In my mind, these two things were intertwined and essential to the success of all Rangers and the Ranger Battalion, but most especially to the Ranger leaders.

When I consider the total fitness of an individual or an organization, I look at its four components: physical, mental, emotional, and spiritual. This is what it takes to lead on the tough days. Now, I plan to discuss my leader approach to the most basic one, physical fitness.

Physical fitness was a routine part of Ranger life, and physical training (PT) was its daily starting point. Normally every day started at 6:30 a.m. on the field with the battalion in formation ready to physically train for the next sixty to ninety minutes. This training was so important because it established the atmosphere for total fitness. It was a routine basic training event that ensured everyone was prepared to answer the tip-of-the-spear call whenever it came, be it on short-notice or no-notice. The normal training session was always exciting, adventuresome, and challenging in some way.

Most important, it was the right training that focused on the concept of making every Ranger better prepared to perform successfully in combat. I did not dictate the daily physical training requirements because that was the responsibility of the subordinate leaders—officers and non-commissioned officers who understood my training guidance very well. My only input into the basic training routines required that every exercise focused on fighting in combat and succeeding every time. Failing in combat is never an option. Providing guidance like this is important, but the understanding and execution of such guidance is what really matters. I was blessed with the finest subordinate leaders any commander could ever have, and they executed the guidance superbly.

My leader approach to physical training revolved around my belief that I must be able to do everything my Rangers could do and do it with them. I had expressed this belief that day I took command in February, so now it was time to show I meant what I said and start earning their respect through actions, not words. The importance of physical training was the same for me, the Battalion Commander, as it was for any Ranger. Regardless of the age of the Battalion Commander (I was forty-two) or the youngest Ranger in the Battalion (many were only eighteen), the same Ranger standards applied to everyone. I would normally get in the office around 5:00 am in order to have some quiet time to organize my day. About 6:15 am I would walk out to the PT field where the battalion was preparing for physical training. After the playing of Reveille and reciting the Ranger Creed, another exciting Ranger-type day was underway. I would then move to join an element with which I had not recently done PT, usually a squad (12 Rangers) or a platoon (45 Rangers). I never knew exactly what the respective squad or platoon PT session was going to entail, but I knew it would be challenging training that I must be able to complete with them. As I approached them, I could often hear some of them mumbling. After four or five weeks I finally figured out what was being said "here comes the old man to go with us today, let's see if we can kill him," etc. They were so interested because they remembered my comments from the day I assumed command and were eager to challenge me. There is one very simple truth about our American soldiers—they are the "smartest" people on the face of the earth because their brilliance is not only in the mind but also in the heart. The humorous view of a soldier's memory would be something like this: soldiers will remember everything they are told—at least what they *want* to remember.

A normal physical training session always included a good solid run of between three and six miles with a pace of seven minutes per mile, plus or minus fifteen seconds. Thus a normal five-mile run would take between thirty-five and thirty-six minutes. This was considered to be a pretty hefty pace for the average Ranger, but especially for the 42-year old Battalion Commander (or so my men thought). Amazingly, when I did PT with any Ranger element, the run pace would always better the seven-minute standard, usually as fast as a 6:45 mile. And instead of the usual three to four mile distance, we often pushed to five or six miles. All the Rangers wanted to push it a little harder than normal to see if the Battalion Commander really could do it with them; they wondered if I could "hang?" In a humorous sort of way, they were trying to "kill" me, or at least hurt me a little—and that was all right. I even had this idea confirmed by one of my former Ranger Sergeants when he heard me speak in Portland, Oregon. There was an informal challenge to see who could "hurt the old man worst, first." You have to love their spirit, HOOAH!

Well, they did not kill me, even though there were a few times after a PT session when I walked into my office, shut the door, and said to myself, "They won, I think I might die right here, right now." Of course I never shared that with them and, thank goodness, they did not kill me, but it was as big a deal to them, as it was to me, to be able to do what they did and do it with them, every time.

*    *    *    *

Once a month it was the Battalion Commander's turn to lead PT. Every training event of any kind always had stated tasks, conditions, and standards, which when executed correctly would result in success. Thus, it was critical to ensure that they were understood by everyone participating. There are however occasions when deviating from the norm can be very beneficial to those being trained, but you must always ensure there is a realistic purpose.

In July 1994, about a week before I was to relinquish command of 3rd Ranger Battalion, I led the PT for the last time. On this occasion I chose not to provide the tasks, conditions, and standards prior to the morning of the actual PT session—very much out of the norm for me. I did this because there was a very important lesson I wanted to leave with them: be prepared for everything and always expect the unexpected.

This was a lesson that was magnified in Mogadishu, Somalia during the mission on October 3–4, 1993. On this very hot, humid July 1994 morning at Fort Benning (one of the hottest, most humid places in the United States), we started our PT session as usual—

warm-up exercises and reciting of the Ranger Creed. After this I said, "Now you are probably wondering what the rest of today's PT session is going to involve since I have not told you the tasks, conditions, and standards yet ... well, I have done that for a reason, and the reason is I want you all to be prepared for everything and always expect the unexpected, and to do so you must be totally fit—physically, mentally, emotionally, and spiritually—and I believe you are totally fit, individually and as a unit. So, let's go do a really good 3rd Ranger Battalion run, HOOAH!" They would HOOAH back vigorously and off we went on the last Battalion Commander-led run.

We started the run by doing our normal route for about the first four miles, but then the unexpected happened, and instead of turning left as usual at the route's T-intersection, we turned right. We were now crossing the Chattahoochee River bridge into Alabama, which meant we could run a really long way. For example, one of the drop zones for airborne operations (Fryar Drop Zone) at Fort Benning was about ten miles out from that T-intersection. Well, after negotiating the first major hill on the route, I decided to run around the battalion formation and see how everyone was doing so far. What I observed were eyes big in amazement, but everyone still running in formation. We reached the turn-around point for the run (ten miles) and it was evident by the looks that most knew we had about ten miles more to go in order to return to the battalion area. Shortly after the ten mile turn, I stopped the battalion run—it was over.

Out of eight hundred-plus Rangers on the run, only two were not standing at the finish. One was a young Ranger who had only been in the battalion about three months, and probably wasn't well acclimatized to the heat and humidity, but he had made it over seven miles before he had to stop, and he was fine. Now, the other Ranger who was not completely standing at the finish was very special—he was my Battalion Chaplain. He went down right after we stopped at mile ten—so he actually completed the run. His recollection of finishing the run was somewhat fuzzy, since he had collapsed moments after the run ended. CH David Moran did recover but it took him five days in Fort Benning's Martin Army Hospital to do so. We are actually very good friends still today, even though I almost killed him. As a matter of fact, he and another former 3rd Ranger Battalion Chaplain officiated at my wedding to Linda in Cocoa, Florida on March 11, 2006. Oh, and by the way, when we finished at the ten mile mark, I had juice, water, coffee, and some munchy food items brought down a side road for all the Rangers … and also, buses to take them back to the battalion area. It was a great day for all of us. They proved they were totally fit and could handle the unexpected, and made me more proud than I could ever express.

\*     \*     \*     \*

There was another regular training opportunity that I felt was critically important to the total fitness of the Ranger Battalion. It was always challenging, dangerous, and demanding for every Ranger—an airborne operation. This training required tactical and technical proficiency, as well as total fitness, of each and every Ranger, but especially of the Ranger officers and non-commissioned officers. Jumping out of an airplane moving 130 knots at approximately 1200 feet above the ground is not a normal human endeavor. I have executed over eighty jumps in my career and I had the same butterflies on the last one in June 1994 that I had on the first one in December 1973, but despite the obvious danger, I was always confident when jumping because I trusted the equipment, the Rangers around me, and the leaders in charge.

Airborne training was critical to our operational capabilities and our mission requirements. Based on the philosophy of *"training the way you will fight in combat because you will fight the way you have trained,"* most of our airborne operations were executed in darkness, because you will almost never conduct a combat airborne operation during daylight hours. For example, the 75th Ranger Regiment's combat airborne assault in Panama on December 20, 1989, was executed at 1:03 am. Jumps that occur in daylight hours are generally considered "proficiency jumps," which seldom occur.

If it was important enough for my Rangers to be conducting nighttime airborne operations, then it was important enough for me to be jumping with them as often as possible. I did not do this because I had to do it, but I did it because I thought it made a difference to my subordinates in that my presence probably made them understand more about the importance of the training. I felt it made a greater difference to the younger Rangers more than anybody else; by showing them their leader really cared and would do everything with them. I remember several occasions when we were hooked-up and ready to jump, and a young Ranger would be looking around uneasily. Then he would see me, and I would give him a positive nod of my head, smile, and say, "Rangers Lead The Way." It usually worked to give him confidence, and he would jump out of that aircraft exuding the Ranger spirit.

★　★　★　★

I wish I could say I was so smart that I knew this leadership and training philosophy would be critically important during something like the situation of October 3–4, 1993, in Mogadishu, Somalia. Well, I have to admit I never foresaw such a thing. I knew the philosophy was important because I had learned about it from the great leaders that I worked for in my career, and because of that training my Rangers knew I was there for them through any adversity. Leading in that Mogadishu operation would have been much more difficult had I not been leading by example since February 1993.

So, what does all of this mean? It means leading is dynamic, not easy, but pretty simple. It means leaders are made, not just born to lead. It means there are good leaders and bad leaders, and what determines the two types are the understanding of the values of LDRSHIP, the personal and professional commitment to your subordinates, the responsibility and accountability for your actions as well as the actions of those you lead, trusting your subordinates as you want them to trust you, and the willingness to make *hard right* decisions when necessary. It is ultimately necessary to remember the idea of honesty when leading others successfully and effectively, and this will quite often lead to political incorrectness. I believe great leaders are willing to be politically incorrect because they are most interested in taking care of those they lead while accomplishing the mission.

The adverse impacts of political correctness on decision-making by leaders will far too often lead to a disastrous result in the execution of a mission. This simple idea of political correctness versus political incorrectness was of major importance in the events commonly referred to now as Black Hawk Down.

# Somalia Mission Background | 4

Let us now look at leadership as applied to an event in military history, which simply means applying the values, concepts, and principles discussed previously to a real world incident. I want to do this by taking you back to the period of December 1992 to October 1993—the place is the East African country of Somalia, and specifically the city of Mogadishu.

Mogadishu lies on the coastline of Somalia and the Indian Ocean, and was the most vital focus of activity for the entire country during this period. The country of Somalia had been devastated by a civil war that resulted in the downfall of the government in 1991, a dictatorial government that was led and controlled by Mohamed Siad Barre. In the absence of any true government, various territories were controlled by those who exerted power forcefully. Many clans wanted to be in control, with no one successful. Thus, the battle was constant, the fighting unending, brutal, ugly, and deadly. Moreover, the lack of any governmental control was exacerbated by a terrible famine during the same time. The combination of these two horrendous situations had led the country and people to the brink of genocide.

In December 1992, President George H. Bush rightfully determined that a humanitarian effort was necessary in Somalia to avoid the total genocide of the Somali people. Just prior to Christmas 1992, a sizeable force of United States Marines went ashore in Mogadishu as the United States-led humanitarian effort got underway. This initial insertion into Mogadishu by the Marines was done under the cover of darkness, as this would facilitate an arrival with the smallest signature and minimize possible resistance. The only difficulty encountered by the Marines upon landing was with the media.

Astonishingly, the media were on the beach with lights and cameras going full blast. Clearly, someone was willing to leak information regarding the Marines' arrival, which is a situation that occurs far too often. Somehow, the concept of an insertion under the "cover of darkness" was meaningless to the media, regardless of the dire jeopardy it created for the Marines. However, their proficiency and professionalism ensured their success. For the many months following, the Marines were very successful in providing security for the much needed humanitarian relief; food, clothing, medical supplies along with medical care were now getting to the people. On or about May 15, 1993, the last Marines who were part of the humanitarian effort departed Mogadishu, and the relief effort was turned over to a United Nations force currently in Mogadishu.

Things were about to change.

On June 5, 1993, approximately three weeks after the Marines had departed, there was a massacre of twenty-four United Nations

Pakistani soldiers in the streets of Mogadishu. They were brutally and savagely killed by the forces of Mohamed Farah Aidid, the leader of the most powerful clan. This massacre of UN soldiers carried with it a message from Aidid to the United Nations: the UN was to leave Mogadishu so Aidid could become the "Ruler" of Somalia. Aidid had been a very powerful general in the Somali Army before the government fell in 1991, and now he wanted to be the Dictator of the country.

This June 5th occurrence was the genesis for what would become known as Task Force RANGER.

*　　*　　*　　*

Now we can start looking at some of the factors that impacted Task Force RANGER in the execution of the mission in Somalia from August to October 1993. These various factors can be analyzed in many ways, such as technically and tactically; however, the most important analysis to me is that of leadership challenges. Interestingly enough, some of the most significant challenges in leadership had to be confronted prior to the Task Force actually deploying to Somalia in late August 1993.

It is crucially important to establish my position about the idea of political correctness: I believe it inevitably leads us down the road of leadership dishonesty and failure. It allows leaders to make the *easy wrong* decision, to compromise integrity, and quite often to show little or no respect for those they lead. I believe the honest and successful leader will more often than not choose the path of political incorrectness which leads to *hard right* decisions, steadfast integrity, and absolute respect at all times for those they are leading.

I have witnessed leaders being politically correct above all else and the results were neither good nor right. In the 1960s, if political correctness had not dominated the decision-making process associated with the Vietnam War, the results would surely have been different. The Vietnam War was necessary in order to stop the spread of Communism in the world at that time, and was the right thing to do. However, the war was controlled more by politically correct decision-making than militarily correct decision-making, and the war resulted in limited success at best and, at worst, far too many Americans dead. The awful political correctness of the Vietnam War had a devastating impact on our military for the next decade, and on our nation as a whole.

So I claim to be one of the most politically incorrect people in the United States of America, and very proud of it. My thoughts on political correctness versus incorrectness have nothing to do with any specific political party; they simply have to do with the ideas of honesty, respect, integrity, and decision-making. As I discuss that August–October period in 1993, I feel certain you will understand my position relating to leadership and this issue of correctness.

★　★　★　★

During the period from December 1992 to May 1993 there were a few minor skirmishes between the Marines and some of Aidid's forces, but nothing of any major consequence. This was because Aidid knew the sizeable Marine force there would have destroyed his clan fighters and subsequently destroyed him and his dream of ruling Somalia. Clearly, Aidid understood his capabilities and chose to wait until this U.S. Marine force had departed Somalia to continue his pursuit for absolute power. And so he did. Approximately three weeks after the departure of the Marines, Aidid attacked the UN military force. He believed this brutal attack on the UN force would cause them to pack up and leave Mogadishu, thus giving him the ability to take over as the most powerful leader in Somalia. This was a realistic strategy, and illustrates why political-military organizations like the United Nations are prone to failure. The UN operates with force in an interesting way—that is to be kind and gentle, which seldom works in military confrontations, most especially in a brutal environment such as Mogadishu, Somalia in 1993. But in this case, Aidid was not prepared for the decisive response of the United Nations.

The UN reacted by establishing a General Resolution declaring that Mohamed Farah Aidid and his forces were responsible for the June 5th attack on the UN Pakistani soldiers, and that they must be brought to justice. The specific nature of this mission was further delineated in the UN General Resolution to include the capture of Mohamed Farah Aidid. It is critically important to understand that this mission as it related to Aidid was a "capture only" mission, which is much more difficult than a "capture or kill" mission (as was the case with Saddam Hussein in Iraq in 2003). This is so because you are operationally limited from a tactical perspective. In essence, you need to be more gentle when attacking a target so as not to kill the "capture only" person or persons.

One other important point regarding the Resolution: it was not protected as a top secret mission. Well kept secrets are not a UN strength, and within a short period of time the mission to capture Aidid became general knowledge. Aidid himself was probably informed of the mission within a few days; thus, from the outset, the mission was extremely difficult and posed much deadlier challenges for our American soldiers. However, at least Aidid did not know who was coming to capture him and when they would attempt to do it. The involvement of the United States, and specifically the U.S. military, in the execution of this mission would make all the difference.

# Task Force RANGER Alert | 5

The new Clinton administration of January 1993 volunteered to provide a U.S. military force to accomplish the UN mission as established in the General Resolution. Thus was created what became known as Task Force RANGER. In the weeks following, the decision to provide a U.S. military force was further refined by assigning the mission to the US Special Operations Command which would then give the actual mission execution requirement to the Joint Special Operations Command (commanded by Major General William Garrison).

The first thing necessary in the operational planning for the execution of this mission was to determine how the mission could best be accomplished and what assets were necessary to accomplish it. In order to do this, it was critical to have all possible intelligence information on the Mogadishu-Aidid situation, and a good tactical reconnaissance conducted of the Mogadishu area. These two things were accomplished and the specifics regarding the structure of Task

Force RANGER were the result. The "how" and "what" necessary to accomplish the mission had been answered sufficiently, and a deployment date to Somalia for the resulting Task Force was then set as on or about (o/a) August 25, 1993. The next important step was to assemble the force at one location in order to plan the execution in detail and rehearse the mission execution to perfection.

★  ★  ★  ★

There are three maneuver Ranger Battalions in the U.S. Army, all of which belong to the 75th Ranger Regiment, which is part of the United States Special Operations Command. Each of the Ranger Battalions was commanded by a Lieutenant Colonel and worked directly for the Ranger Regimental Commander. The Ranger Battalions are located at three different military installations: 1st Ranger Battalion at Hunter Army Airfield, Savannah, Georgia; 2nd Ranger Battalion at Fort Lewis, Seattle-Tacoma, Washington; and 3rd Ranger Battalion at Fort Benning, Columbus, Georgia (also the headquarters of the Ranger Regiment, commanded by a colonel). These three Ranger Battalions, along with some other integral but smaller elements, comprise the U.S. Army's one and only Ranger Regiment (the 75th Ranger Regiment). Each battalion must maintain an extraordinarily high level of combat readiness three hundred sixty-five days a year. One of the three battalions is always designated as the Ranger Ready Force 1 (RRF1) battalion, and will be in that RRF1 status for a two-month period. Thus, each battalion will be the RRF1 battalion twice during the calendar year.

When a battalion is in the RRF1 status, it means it has both the responsibility and the ability to deploy as a combat force anywhere in the world within eighteen hours after initial alert notification, a state of readiness commonly referred to as being on a "short string." In the case of 3rd Ranger Battalion (3/75 Rgr Bn), this short string limited the Rangers to traveling generally not more than fifty miles from Fort Benning for the two months they were in RRF1 status. This was fairly restrictive, but clearly understood by the Rangers... a realistic perspective on this might simply be that the Rangers enjoyed RRF1 because it meant if something did happen in the world *they* were going to be called on first. This attitude is not sadistic; it is actually highly conducive to success because a Ranger is my idea of an extreme type-A personality individual—someone who wants to be called on to go first. A Ranger Battalion soldier is an absolute total volunteer because he has volunteered multiple times to get there; he has volunteered for the Army, volunteered for Airborne School, and volunteered to be in a Ranger Battalion.

I was blessed to be the Commander of such a special unit ... all volunteers who wanted to be there and wanted to be at the "tip of the spear." I proudly and confidently say the three Ranger Battalions comprise the most responsive battalion-size combat force the Army has today, and along with the numerous other units in the special operations force structure, they comprise the finest fighting force anywhere in the world.

★　★　★　★

In June–July 1993, 3rd Ranger Battalion was the Ranger Regiment's RRF1 Battalion, but a unique situation existed when the battalion was to come off the RRF1 status. It was scheduled to be a major participant in a joint special operations exercise during the

August-September 1993 time period that required the entire battalion to deploy to Fort Bliss in El Paso, Texas for training prior to the start of the exercise. Even though we were not the RRF1 Battalion in August 1993, we were extremely well prepared to deploy since we had just concluded our rotation, and as a Ranger Battalion you were always expected to be ready to deploy anytime, anywhere. But realistically, could you possibly execute a real-world deployment if you were already deployed away from home station (Fort Benning in our case)? Very simply: yes.

This is so because you would deploy for the training exercise just like you would deploy for a real-world mission ... minus your combat basic-load of ammunition, which could be sent to you before any mission deployment. This is the basis for the simple training philosophy, "train the way you want to fight in combat because you will fight in combat the way you have trained."

On August 3, 1993, 3rd Ranger Battalion conducted an airborne operation that took it from Fort Benning to Fort Bliss where it would train in preparation for the upcoming exercise. The exact start date of the exercise was not known at the time, as that was part of the exercise process to alert the respective units and react on short notice. The airborne operation of August 3rd was very memorable for me since it was the 20th anniversary of my being in the U.S. Army. What a great anniversary event! It was my first time at Fort Bliss and I found El Paso to be a very interesting area. The landscape was quite barren but it was a fantastic training area with the White Sands Missile Range and Roswell, New Mexico nearby.

The living arrangements for everyone were pretty standard—cots inside general purpose medium tents with no air conditioning. After "jumping in" on August 3rd, we immediately started the training regimen, doing numerous things to prepare for the actual training, including equipment preparation and leaders reconnaissance of the training areas. Some elements of 3rd Battalion started training as soon as August 4th with all elements training by August 5th. The Battalion's training was going very well; training highlights included airfield seizure operations and various live-fire exercises. On August 7th, the Regimental Headquarters (my boss's headquarters element) deployed to Fort Bliss from Fort Benning in preparation for the upcoming exercise. By August 8th, the 2nd Ranger Battalion, the other operational Ranger Battalion for the exercise, had deployed from Fort Lewis to Fort Bliss in preparation. Thus, all the Ranger elements were deployed to Fort Bliss and were training by the 10th of August. The 1st Ranger Battalion had assumed the RRF1 status.

*   *   *   *

On August 10th I was out participating in some live-fire exercises with one of my units when I was informed that the Regimental Commander needed to see me. This was a little disturbing to me as it meant I would have to leave the training area and return to the cantonment area to meet with my boss; I was hesitant about leaving training in the middle of such an exercise, but I begrudgingly returned as directed. I soon met with the Regimental Commander (RCO) who informed me about a real-world mission alert. My initial response to him was, "Is this real-world, real-world or real-world exercise?" I asked this question because I was unaware of any real-world hot spots at the time, and furthermore, we were about to execute a major training exercise that was very close to being real-world in nature. But the RCO made it clear this was a real-world, real-world situation, not part of the training exercise.

My next questions were: where are we going? What are we going to be doing? When do we leave? My boss's responses were that he could only tell me that I would be departing from Fort Bliss the next day. An answer to only one out of my three questions was not a good start, I thought; the RCO knew I was looking for answers regarding the real-world mission, but he did not have that information at the time. What he did have was alert notification information only, not mission-specific top-secret level information. I reiterated my questions, and asked when we would leave tomorrow, where would we be going, and what would we be doing there? The RCO then told me that we would be deploying to Fort Bragg, North Carolina, where we would join other Special Operations forces, receive our real-world mission briefing, train for the mission, then deploy to the real-world mission area of operation from Fort Bragg.

This information actually told me a great deal because in the Special Operations community a real-world train-up at Fort Bragg would normally mean training with SFOD-D (Delta Force) at their respective location. The SFOD-D training facility is one-of-a-kind and allows for a full mission train-up under the finest and most secure training conditions. Furthermore, this slight bit of information told me something about the mission force structure; if a Ranger Battalion and SFOD-D were going to be involved, then the Special Operations Aviation unit, Task Force 160, from Fort Campbell, Kentucky, would most likely be there too.

Therefore, at this point, I knew where I was going the next day and what would follow upon arriving at Fort Bragg; I just did not know any mission specifics. My next question was critically important … what do I take with me? I had the entire battalion there at

Fort Bliss, and hoped to take all eight hundred fifty Rangers. My boss's response was that I would take one rifle company (generally one hundred ninety Rangers), one additional platoon (forty-five to fifty Rangers), and a few staff personnel. This meant that my piece of the combat force would be about two hundred forty Rangers—not a large fighting force.

Again, based on past experience with SFOD-D and TF160, I could reasonably determine that the approximate size of the total force for this mission would be roughly five hundred plus personnel. The size and make-up of the total force was also very important information because it was somewhat indicative of the mission type. With this total force, the mission would be relatively small in terms of the target—probably a building facility or vehicle convoy to capture or kill someone. If the mission were much more involved, I would normally take at least two rifle companies.

★　★　★　★

I now had to determine, based only on this limited information, which soldiers to bring from the battalion. First criterion was timeliness: a timely, quick decision on who would be the mission force was critical because there was less than twenty-four hours before the force would be deployed from Fort Bliss to Fort Bragg, and whoever was deploying was currently out in the field training. Once I made the decision on who was going and informed them, they would have to return to the Fort Bliss cantonment area and start the deployment process: packing, cleaning and loading of equipment on the respective aircraft for the movement to Fort Bragg. Timeliness of the decision was therefore crucial.

The second consideration, and probably the most important reason in my making the decision alone, was my knowledge of the battalion's subordinate unit capabilities. From February 11, when I took command, to this time in August, I had learned the battalion very well, from individual leaders to the squads to the platoons to the companies. My knowledge of the battalion was based on numerous things; however, most important to my confidence in knowing their capabilities was the simple fact that I had trained with them on a routine basis. The process to select the mission force was simple, but the actual selection was difficult because the personnel and the units all merited inclusion in the mission.

⋆    ⋆    ⋆    ⋆

Now to the actual process and the selection of the mission force. There were three Ranger rifle companies in the battalion—Alpha Company, Bravo Company and Charlie Company. From these three, I had to choose one to be the primary company. I quickly eliminated Charlie Company because the Company Commander (Captain) had only been in command a little over thirty days at this point. He had not yet been involved in a tough, stressful training opportunity with the company, which was necessary to earn the type of trust, confidence and respect needed to lead in combat. The pending exercise would definitely provide him such an opportunity to prove these important elements of command to all, especially with his subordinates. The company was the typical outstanding Ranger rifle company, and the Commander was a fine officer, but timing was not right for them. So, I was now left with the choice of one of two.

Again, as with Charlie Company, I saw two typically outstanding Ranger rifle companies. I saw two very experienced Company Commanders who had been in command for about six months, both performing superbly on a daily basis. My next check was to look at the right-hand person to the Company Commander—the Company First Sergeant. The First Sergeant is the senior non-commissioned officer (sergeant level ranks) in the Ranger company, and what I saw was two very solid leaders who performed exceptionally well on a routine basis. One was slightly more experienced than the other, but not to a significant degree. I had actually looked at the positions of Company Commander and First Sergeant in Alpha and Bravo companies just to ensure that there were no shortcomings— there were none—and that the leadership experience was nothing less than top-notch, and it was. Furthermore, I was only allowed to take one company plus one platoon from another company. To me this meant the mission would most likely involve small unit combat operations.

This type of combat would generally focus on platoon operations, so I looked at the platoon level leadership of both companies. A platoon is led by a platoon leader (Lieutenant) and a platoon sergeant (Sergeant First Class), and there are forty-five to fifty Rangers in a platoon. My initial look at the platoons (four per company) was focused on the Platoon Leaders. When I looked at the Lieutenant Platoon Leaders, I was confronted with an interesting but good problem: they were all absolutely outstanding. The norm is that a Ranger Battalion Commander must have commanded a regular Army battalion for a year or so before being selected to command a Ranger battalion, and a Ranger Company Commander must have commanded a regular Army company for a year or so before any selection to command a Ranger company. This hierarchy is based on experience and getting the best of the best to lead in Ranger units.

The Ranger Platoon Leaders were selected in much the same manner as the Battalion and Company Commanders—at least one year as a platoon leader, a superb performance rating for that year, and a volunteer to come to the Ranger battalion. All my 3rd Battalion Lieutenants were experienced leaders, fine officers, and terrific soldiers—truly the best of the best. I was blessed to have such a good problem; thus, the platoon leader position did not provide me with a decision point. It should be noted that the ones that did go to Somalia performed beyond any reasonable expectations and continued to do so afterwards in our Army, with two of them going on to become leaders in the Special Operations Delta Force unit.

So, still needing to make the decision on whom to deploy, I looked at the Platoon Sergeants in these two companies (Alpha and Bravo). The Platoon Sergeant (an experienced Sergeant First Class) is the right-hand person to the Platoon Leader just as the First Sergeant is to the Company Commander. The Platoon Sergeants (four in the company) in both these companies were as good as I had ever seen in my career, both individually and as a group. Yes, once again I was confronted with this good problem of selecting from the best of the best. I made the selection at this point—not an easy thing, but done. My company selection was Bravo Company, based on the Platoon Sergeants. Of the four Platoon Sergeants in B Company, all four had been in combat with Special Operations units in Panama in 1989-90 during Operation JUST CAUSE. These four were experienced combat leaders, which gave me great confidence especially since I was preparing for an unknown mission.

So Bravo Company was selected as the primary company, and one platoon was selected from A Company (another combat experienced Platoon Sergeant). If I made one really good decision during all the happenings associated with Task Force RANGER and the respective mission in Somalia, it was that of taking the right people, especially at the leader levels, and even more so basing it on Platoon Sergeants. I say this not only because they were superb combat leaders in September–October 1993, but because they have continued to be great leaders during subsequent years. They continued to serve in our Army, and all attained the rank of Sergeant Major. Furthermore, each one was designated as Command Sergeant Major and led soldiers in combat as a battalion and/or brigade Command Sergeant Major in Iraq and/or Afghanistan in the years following September 11, 2001.

Having completed the initial decision-making process, it was now time to gather the deploying Ranger force and brief them on what I knew, and prepare for the movement to Fort Bragg the next day.

# The Mission: Initial Preparation and Rehearsal | 6

After the decision on the composition of the Ranger fighting force, the two hundred forty Ranger personnel were assembled within a few hours for their briefing. An hour earlier I had the officers and senior NCOs assembled for my initial briefing to them. Additionally, I had to brief the leadership that would be staying at Fort Bliss for the exercise about their status and provide guidance for them. A very important item covered in detail was that of Operational Security (OPSEC). No discussion of a pending mission or deployment to Fort Bragg could take place. This applied to those going to Fort Bragg as well as those staying at Fort Bliss. Phone calls back to Fort Benning, especially to family members, could result in a major security leak. Therefore, the decision was made to cease all phone calls by anyone in 3rd Battalion without specific approval from me or my Battalion Executive Officer. This "no call" status did not change until after the arrival of Task Force RANGER in Somalia on August 26, 1993. This restriction was not unusual; as a matter of fact, it was normal during a training deployment to implement this as part of the training.

After all the personnel were briefed, it was time to clean up and pack up all equipment that would be going to Fort Bragg, then get some rest. After a relatively short night of rest, we flew to North Carolina, arriving early on the evening on August 11th.

After arriving at Fort Bragg, we moved to the SFOD-D (Delta Force) compound where leaders of the 3rd Ranger Battalion element received the mission briefing, as well as the training/rehearsal plan for the mission. The specific mission was to deploy to Mogadishu, Somalia to capture the most powerful warlord there—Mohamed Farah Aidid—as well as any of his key leaders.

At last we knew what we would be doing and where, and that it was going to occur within the next few weeks. The other units/personnel that would become part of what was to be known as Task Force RANGER had also assembled at the SFOD-D compound. Now it was time for our highly intense training and mission rehearsals to take place. These were designed for the "capture only" mission of Mohamed Farah Aidid and his key leaders. The operational scenarios for the mission focused on attacking a building/facility in a city or attacking a vehicular convoy. These were routine scenarios, but were more difficult in this case due to the "capture only" nature of the UN mission.

The key to successful mission execution is always based on intense, realistic training and precise mission rehearsals, which is exactly what was done at Fort Bragg from August 12–22 by Task Force RANGER. This tremendous Task Force of Special Operations personnel—from Delta Force, TF160 Aviation, 3rd Ranger Battalion, and other specialized elements such as Air Force Pararescue (PJs) and Combat Control personnel and Navy Seals—was trained and ready to deploy in about ten days. It should also be noted that the Air Force was involved with its AC-130 gunship, a significant fire support element for Special Operations missions on many occasions. On August 22, after ten-plus days of intense training and precise mission rehearsals, Task Force RANGER was prepared and ready for deployment to Mogadishu, Somalia.

*   *   *   *

In my opinion, the date of August 22, 1993 was one of the really significant dates associated with the mission to Somalia that would later be named Operation GOTHIC SERPENT. On this date, we were informed that a decision had been made to cancel the mission to Somalia; GOTHIC SERPENT was a *no-go*. Any and all elements of the Task Force associated with the Fort Bliss exercise, such as those from 3rd Ranger Battalion, were to pack up and prepare to return to Fort Bliss to rejoin it. There was no explanation for the cancellation except that some things had changed and that was about all we were told. As a leader, one understands things can change and missions may be postponed or even cancelled on occasion. I had seen this occur previously, but never after a ten-plus day train-up with specific mission rehearsals. Something just did not seem right about this decision, but it had been made, and we needed to get on with the new task of returning to Fort Bliss.

The first thing I had to do after being informed of this decision was to get my subordinate leaders together and brief them; they did not like it, but also understood that things change. Next I had to get all my Rangers together and inform them of this decision. This was a leadership challenge because there were two hundred-plus Rangers trained and ready to execute a real world Special Operations mission with the best Special Operations soldiers in the world, and they were excited about this opportunity. These young men volunteered to come to a Ranger unit because they wanted to be part of the best and be at the tip of the spear. They expected to go to combat; they wanted to go to combat; their time had come, and they were jacked up about it.

Now I had to tell them their time was not here yet.

When I briefed them on the mission cancellation, I remember their disappointment. It was exactly what I had expected and had prepared myself for. I felt it was imperative to handle this situation in a totally positive manner; nothing else would have been acceptable. If I allowed these Rangers, especially the younger ones, to feel so disappointed that they became unfocused upon returning to Fort Bliss, just participating in live-fire exercises could be a matter of life or death. So I told them returning to Fort Bliss and the on-going exercise was going to be a unique challenge for them, but certainly different from the last twelve or so days.

I actually tried to challenge them because they wanted a challenge. I told them they had just had some of the most realistic, tough training anyone could possibly have had and that they were better trained than anyone in the Special Operations force to do the specific mission they had been given. Furthermore, if this type mission was to come up again in the near future, I was certain that they would be called on to execute it. Finally, they were going back to the Fort Bliss exercise much better trained than they had been before arriving at Fort Bragg on August 11. Oh yes, a mission similar to what they had been training for could present itself during the exercise, and if so, it would be theirs to execute. Now I said I expected from them nothing less than perfect execution.

*   *   *   *

Now they had a new challenge, and the look in their eyes said *bring it on, we are ready*. Then my subordinate leaders took it from there and made things happen in the right way. Remember, leaders can never afford to have a bad day with their soldiers; they must be positive at all times. Late on the 22nd, early on the 23rd, we boarded the airplanes and flew back to Fort Bliss, Texas. Upon our arrival, I told the returning Rangers to get their gear squared away, then change into civilian clothes and take a break and go to downtown El Paso for dinner. We had now dealt with a leadership issue in a positive way.

During speaking experiences to many thousands of people across our great country, I have encountered fewer than ten people who were aware the Somalia mission had been canceled on August 22, 1993. There is something very wrong about that fact (must be political correctness at work). The next thought would probably be: wait a minute, you went back to Fort Bliss, but somehow you ended up in Somalia—*how*? Well, we are just getting started, to put it politely, in regard to decision-making.

There are three types of decisions we must consider here: good decisions, bad decisions, and *stupid* decisions. In my opinion we have just dealt with a bad decision—the mission cancellation on August 22—but there were many good decisions prior to that, the most important of which was to give the mission to the appropriate military forces and let them execute it.

Yet, there we were, back at Fort Bliss. My staff personnel brought me up to speed on the exercise and I provided them limited information on the training that had taken place at Fort Bragg while omitting all mission-specific details. While sitting in the Operations tent talking with the staff, the field phone rang and one of my young officers answered it. He said to me, "Sir, it is the Regimental Liaison Officer for you." This officer was a Major who worked in the Regimental Operations Section at the higher headquarters. As I walked to the phone, I casually said, "He's probably calling to tell us the mission is on again."

I was joking when I said it, but when I got on the phone and told him that we were breaking down our equipment to prepare for participation in the exercise, his reply was "Stop. The Regimental Commander is on his way to see you now." Right then, I knew the mission was back on; there was no other logical reason to stop the equipment breakdown. And sure enough, the RCO confirmed that the mission was back on, the deployment to Mogadishu was a *go*, and we were to be on the aircraft for departure at 0700 the next morning.

Another leadership challenge had been presented to me and my subordinate leaders, the challenge to make sense of this very questionable decision-making process. To say it was questionable and bad is probably being kind from my foxhole. From the start of the day on August 22nd to the end of the day on August 23rd, the Somalia mission went from *go* to *no-go* to *go*, which is extremely disruptive to the soldier trying to prepare for action.

My leadership challenge was clear and simple: to prepare the Rangers for re-deployment to Fort Bragg, then on to Somalia for a tough combat mission. This may seem simple on the surface, but it's difficult when dealing with intelligent young Rangers who want things to make sense. It was my leader responsibility to make some sense of it, first to my subordinate leaders, then to every Ranger in Task Force RANGER.

The first order of business was to get all the respective Rangers from downtown El Paso back to the Fort Bliss cantonment area, which was accomplished in short order. After assembling all deploying Rangers at our Fort Bliss area, I simply told them some changes had again occurred in Mogadishu that now made this mission more important than ever. We would be going to combat and it would be within days, not weeks. We needed to get focused and ready to execute the mission. I knew they were physically ready, but I wanted to make sure they were focused mentally as well. This force of about two hundred thirty Rangers understood what needed to be done, accepted the challenge, and redeployed to Fort Bragg ready for the mission in Somalia. It was unfortunate that we were not flying on commercial airlines because we could have really built up the "sky miles" going back and forth across the country—yea, right—HOOAH!

Upon our arrival back at Fort Bragg, I indicated that there were two critical tasks to be accomplished by the Rangers. First, everyone was to prepare themselves and their equipment for the deployment to Somalia that would be occurring within the next twenty-four to thirty-six hours.

Second, I told my subordinate leaders that the Rangers were to go to the firing range as soon as possible. I wanted each deploying Ranger on the range shooting their weapons, in order to facilitate mental focus. I believe there is nothing that will better prepare a soldier for combat than firing his weapon—pulling the trigger, feeling the weapon recoil, and hitting the target. This will get the mindset right. So, not only would this improve their mental focus but it would also improve their shooting proficiency. I have never met anyone who was such a good marksman that they did not need to shoot whenever possible. As a matter of fact, a Delta Force Operator, MSG Gary Gordon, who was a Medal of Honor recipient and as good a shot as I had ever seen, once told me that he would go to the range as often as possible because he always felt he could get a little better.

★   ★   ★   ★

Before proceeding with what was still coming in terms of pre-deployment decisions, let me share some thoughts on the decision-makers, and what had already occurred regarding decisions. The good decision was to assign the mission to our Special Operations Forces. The bad decision was to give the mission a *go/no-go/go* status. The first part of analyzing the decision-making process is to identify the decision-makers. This is actually rather easy because American soldiers had been committed to a combat mission. In almost every case, for American soldiers to be committed to combat, the authorization must have the stamp of approval of the Commander-in-Chief. In January 1993 the United States Presidential Administration changed when the Clinton Administration replaced the Bush Administration and marked the beginning of a tough eight years for the U.S. Armed Forces.

In addition to the necessary involvement of the Commander-in-Chief, certain others had to be involved, some of whom were the Secretary of Defense, the Secretary of State, the National Security

Advisor, and the Chairman of the Joint Chiefs of Staff. Others involved were most likely the Chief of Staff for each respective military service, as well as some military command personnel from the major commands associated with the mission such as USSOCOM and USCENTCOM. Some of the names were President Bill Clinton, Secretary of Defense Les Aspin, Secretary of State Warren Christopher, National Security Advisor Anthony Lake, and Chairman of the Joint Chiefs of Staff General Colin Powell. None of these people are on my Christmas card list because of their allegiance to political correctness at the expense of honesty.

A decision-making flaw had already surfaced in the *go/no-go/go* execution status of the mission and the "changes" that caused this were based on political correctness and inexperience of the decision-makers. One likely change that caused the uncertainty of the mission execution was the lack of total commitment by the Clinton Administration to go through with the mission, even though it had willingly volunteered to do so when the UN established the mission. I believe there was a unilateral attempt by this Administration to back out of the mission, which led to our deployment back to Fort Bliss on August 22-23. Furthermore, I believe this was unacceptable to the UN, and the resulting UN political pressure caused the Clinton Administration to give in and put the mission execution back on—all of which could have been avoided if military decisions had been left to military leaders and not to those who were constrained by the fetters of political correctness.

# The Mission: Final Preparation and STUPID Decisions | 7

The deployment from Fort Bliss back to Fort Bragg went well. The Ranger element of Task Force RANGER was focused and ready for combat operations, and the final stages of preparation for deployment to Somalia were in motion. The leadership of Task Force RANGER from Major General Garrison down had weathered this questionable decision-making process. Task Force RANGER was ready.

Unfortunately for the Task Force, the questionable decision-making was not finished yet; two more decisions—profoundly *stupid* ones—awaited us once we returned to Fort Bragg. They were briefed to the Task Force's key leaders by MG Garrison's stay-behind staff because he and a small group of key personnel had already deployed to Mogadishu prior to our return. Timing-wise, we learned of these decisions only about thirty-six to forty hours prior to our landing on the airfield in Mogadishu, Somalia on the 26th.

The first *stupid* decision was in regards to the size of the Task

Force to deploy to Somalia, which was to be only four hundred fifty personnel. The second *stupid* decision was that no Air Force AC-130 gunship would deploy in support of our mission. These two fatally *stupid* decisions impacted significantly on Task Force RANGER, and especially on the operation that was executed on October 3–4, 1993, in the streets of Mogadishu's Bakara Market area, the most dangerous part of the city.

★　★　★　★

Now let's look at these two *stupid* decisions in some detail. The one that limited the Task Force to four hundred fifty personnel was significant because it caused us to cut approximately one hundred personnel out of the Task Force a mere twenty-four hours prior to deployment. This meant that I had to eliminate the forty-six-man A Company platoon from the Task Force. The Ranger element therefore had to make adjustments in its operational execution of the mission because fewer personnel were available to execute the required tasks. Although each and every Ranger was capable of doing his primary task as well as that of someone else, the elimination of the platoon also meant there was no available reserve force for any operation because almost all personnel were committed on every mission. It is important to have a reserve, and preferably to have one which is totally familiar and synchronized with every aspect of the tactical operation. Obviously now this was no longer the case.

The importance of a reserve force was such that a reasonably suitable alternative was identified and became part of the operational plan for Task Force RANGER. This identified alternative for a reserve force was an infantry unit (battalion) from the 10th Mountain Division already in Mogadishu as part of the United Nations force there; they were the UN's Quick Reaction Force. It was decided that once on the ground in Mogadishu arrangements would be made to coordinate and train with this battalion in case the need for them as a reserve arose during an operation. This was practical because there was a basic compatibility of weapons, communications equipment, vehicles, and operational standards, and those items that may have been unique to our operations would be specifically trained on as needed. Clearly, from the Ranger element perspective, we were a *go* for combat operations in Somalia, despite this *stupid* personnel limitation. It is important to note that the reduction in personnel also impacted other parts of Task Force RANGER, as the Delta Force and the 160th Special Operations Aviation Battalion were forced to make cuts as well.

The fact that this decision was made to limit the size of Task Force RANGER to four hundred fifty personnel is simply mind-boggling, and an example of the worst kind of political correctness. The explanation we were given was that the decision-makers "did not want this to look like a build-up similar to Vietnam." If this was true, it was the most absurd reason imaginable. I am a strong believer in the experts making the really important decisions about the professional aspects of any mission, job, or task. After all, you do not let a lawyer perform surgery.

This poorly made political decision was further exacerbated by the fact that many of the decision-makers involved were not in support of the Vietnam War, including President Clinton. Some of them even chose to protest against the war and avoid being involved in it. To me, for these people to make any comparisons to the Vietnam War was extremely disrespectful toward the great Americans who served their country there. Furthermore, the decision to reduce the Task Force by approximately one hundred personnel was arbitrary and gave the impression that this decision was all about Presidential political control, not military execution. It is difficult to imagine the American public viewing an extra one hundred soldiers as a build-up similar to that which occurred in Vietnam. Additionally, if routine need-to-know operational security had been preserved, then the average American citizen would know little to nothing about Task Force RANGER's mission until it was successfully completed.

*   *   *   *

This reduction in personnel also presented another leadership challenge for me. Now I had to somehow effectively explain to the forty-six non-deploying Rangers in the platoon from A Company why they were not going to Somalia. I first briefed the Platoon Leader and Platoon Sergeant on the capping of the Task Force at four hundred fifty personnel, and that it was my decision to cut them from the Task Force as part of the reduction. The decision to cut these soldiers was a simple one because of unit integrity, as the remainder of my fighting force was essentially all B Company. This part was easily understood by everyone in the platoon, but trying to explain the overall reduction decision was not so easy because it was a *stupid* decision.

The leadership challenge was telling those forty-six Rangers that they would not be a part of the combat mission they had so intensely trained for with their buddies. Try to imagine how they felt being left behind. Try to imagine how they felt on October 3–4 when their Ranger buddies were shot and killed in Mogadishu. They would tell you how awful they felt on both occasions, but their deepest feelings were about the 3$^{rd}$ and 4$^{th}$ of October because they believed that it could have been different if they had been there fighting beside their Ranger buddies, and I agree with them. One of my young Rangers in that forty-six-man platoon, Eric Rosendahl, shared those exact thoughts with me when he and his wife attended my presentation in Portland, Oregon in January 2007. He lives in that area now with his family where he works in the Vancouver, Washington fire department.

After I had briefed the entire platoon, the Platoon leader and Platoon Sergeant took over this leadership challenge. They did a superb job of getting the Rangers focused on their return to Fort Bliss (again) and rejoining the exercise. This was not easy because not deploying with Task Force RANGER was a tremendous letdown to each and every one of the forty-six Rangers in the platoon. These types of leadership challenges are never easy because you are dealing with the leading of people. The one stipulation I made regarding their redeployment to Fort Bliss was that it would not occur until Task Force RANGER was on the ground in Somalia in total. This took a couple of days, which provided what I considered to be very important downtime for them to get focused on rejoining the Fort Bliss exercise. The more specific battlefield impacts of this *stupid* decision will be addressed later.

★   ★   ★   ★

Now for the second *stupid* decision of eliminating the Air Force AC-130 gunship from the Task Force RANGER assets, and the associated impacts.

When a Special Operations mission is executed, it is normally done with tremendous proficiency because of the extraordinary level of training and rehearsals that take place during the preparation phase. Successful mission execution is attributed to this kind of proficiency plus the elements of surprise, speed of action, and violence of action. This simply means that you hit the target/objective hard and fast with everything you have available, and do so with as much surprise as possible. This will almost always result in mission accomplishment.

On the rare occasion that everything does not go as planned, however, there must be an additional part of the plan that can be executed to ensure mission success. In Special Operations missions this quite often means the use of some additional forces (a reserve) or some very specific firepower assets, such as the AC-130 gunship which was part of the initial plan of execution for operations in Somalia by Task Force RANGER. If things did not go exactly as planned and additional firepower was necessary the AC-130 would be there in support. This kind of firepower was needed on October 3rd, and would have made a major difference. Unfortunately, the AC-130 and its crew—who had been part of the planning/rehearsals at Fort Bragg—was not there to be called on because that second *stupid* decision eliminated it from the Task Force package. Now we had a smaller Task Force to operate without a major firepower asset.

The explanation that we were given for this *stupid* decision was that it was about a concern for collateral damage. This concern was supposedly based on the fact that an AC-130 supporting the Marines earlier in the year in Mogadishu (during the humanitarian mission) had caused some collateral damage. My response to this was "So what?" It is my belief that if soldiers are being put in harm's way, then there must be some acceptance of the risk that things like collateral damage can possibly happen. If this acceptance is not possible, then don't place the soldiers there. Another key aspect regarding this *stupid* concern over collateral damage was that a reasonable assessment of Mogadishu by the decision-makers would have revealed that most of the city was already in shambles from the collateral damage of the Somali clan fighting, and the overall civil unrest that had existed for numerous years.

If the decision to reduce the fighting force was stupid, then recalling the AC-130 was catastrophically so. Granted that it was not needed for the target-building takedown or personnel capture operation, nor even to help secure the first downed helicopter which was accomplished by ground elements with AH-6 Little Bird air support. But the AC-130 fire support could have ensured the safety and security of everyone at the site of the second downed helicopter. If we had had this aerial support, I am certain that not only Mike Durant would be alive, but my five fellow soldiers Ray Frank, Tommie Field, Bill Cleveland, Randy Shughart, and Gary Gordon would be as well.

Many attempts were made by the vehicular convoy to move to the second crash site and secure it. Unfortunately, the convoy had incurred a large number of casualties, as well as a loss of some vehicles during its movement toward the first crash site. When the convoy attempted to move to the second crash site, it encountered numerous roadblocks and ambushes that stopped movement to the second downed helicopter. There had even been an attempt made by a small element of Task Force RANGER personnel in HMMWVs from the airfield to find a way to the second crash site, and this too proved to be futile due to the roadblocks and ambushes that were awaiting any and all vehicles. Also, some elements of the 10th Mountain Division's Quick Reaction Force, 2-14th Infantry Battalion, had also been dispatched from the UN Compound to try and reach this second downed helicopter. They made a valiant effort but were also unsuccessful.

★   ★   ★   ★

Another key factor in these tragic events was the involvement—or lack of involvement—of the Chairman of the Joint Chiefs of Staff, General Colin Powell. General Powell was the Chairman when the new Presidential Administration took over in January 1993. He would complete his tenure as the Chairman in the summer of 1993 and planned to retire at that time. The President wanted General Powell to remain for the rest of his tenure, and General Powell agreed to do so. He had served his nation with great honor for well over thirty years; he was a great professional soldier, a phenomenal leader, and a true American patriot. He had always shown a propensity to support military actions in a way that exhibited military strength and power, exemplified by his track record as Chairman with actions in Panama 1989-90 and Kuwait-Iraq in 1991-92. He almost always let professionals do what they were trained to do, and made sure they had all they needed to do the job.

Regrettably, this did not occur in 1993 with Task Force RANGER—so why not? It is actually very simple: when General Colin Powell left his position as Chairman of the Joint Chiefs of Staff in the summer of 1993, the Vice Chairman, Admiral Jeremiah, took over as Acting Chairman. Therefore, General Powell's pending departure during much of the decision-making process regarding

Task Force RANGER and the mission in Somalia resulted in a lack of strong, positive influence from military leadership. The Administration failed to listen to those military recommendations that focused on successful mission accomplishment.

If I were to find a specific fault with the generally awful decision-making process seen here, I would say clearly that the political decision-makers were the ones who must shoulder the blame. I believe this is the ultimate example of political inexperience, political ego and political correctness interfering with simply doing the *hard right* thing. Experienced and professional military leaders should have been allowed to execute this mission as it needed to be done with all the right personnel and all the right assets.

Finally, there have been many Monday morning quarterbacks who have said that maybe we should not have gone at all. I disagree with this thought because as a Task Force we knew we were totally capable of executing this operation and completing the mission. Our mindset was that we could and we would capture Mohamed Farah Aidid. True, we had dealt with many changes and disconcerting situations in the final week before actually deploying to Mogadishu, but the necessary adjustments had been made successfully. Now, the time had arrived for the deployment to Mogadishu and the execution of Operation Gothic Serpent—the capture of Mohamed Farah Aidid.

# Deployment— Finally On The Ground | 8

W ith all the necessary adjustments made by Task Force RANGER, it was finally time to actually deploy to Mogadishu, Somalia, and all elements of the Task Force were on the ground by the 27th of August. However, upon arrival some more interesting, challenging and unnecessary things awaited us. When the aircraft I was on landed, it was time for me to once again confront an uncomfortable and challenging situation. As I was gathering my gear and preparing to get off, I noticed someone from the United Nations element board the aircraft (wearing the UN baby blue beret). Initially, I did not pay that much attention, but that changed when I heard the person say "Is LTC McKnight here?"

Now I was paying attention. My response was, "Yes, right here. What do you need?" He first introduced himself, "Sir, my name is MAJ David Stockwell, and I am a Public Affairs Officer with the UN." This meant he was a media relations person, which gave me a very uneasy feeling. I asked him what he needed with me and he responded by telling me MG Garrison had been briefed and directed me to handle this matter. He then proceeded to tell me that I must get off the plane with him first in order to conduct an interview with the media who were outside awaiting our arrival. My immediate response was, "What do you mean the media is waiting out there? How do they even know of our deployment?" In a rather defensive and somewhat apologetic manner, he told me that our departure from Fort Bragg had made the national news. Somehow, someone had leaked the information regarding Task Force RANGER and its mission to Somalia.

And if the mainstream American media knew we were there, then it was almost certainly known by Mohamed Farah Aidid.

It is important to recall the security measures taken by everyone in 3rd Ranger Battalion once the Somalia mission was given to us on August 10th. These security measures were adhered to with vigilance by the Rangers, both those assigned to the mission and those remaining for the exercise at Fort Bliss. The best example of our security emphasis can be noted in the case of a young Ranger by the name of Jason Coleman. Jason was a Specialist Four in Bravo Company, the deploying company. He was an outstanding young Ranger in his early twenties. After our return to Fort Bragg from Fort Bliss for the deployment to Somalia, Jason approached me and asked me if I thought we would be back from Somalia before the end of September. I told him that would really be pushing it, then asked him why it was important. Jason said his wedding date was in late September. After a moment's thought, I looked at this fine young Ranger and told him he would probably not make his wedding.

Jason then asked if he could call his bride-to-be and tell her there was a need to postpone the wedding. I had to make the *hard right* decision to tell Jason he could not call her at all because of security concerns; if he were to call and tell her to postpone the wedding, he could not tell her the truth, nor probably give her any believable explanation at all. Jason had set the wedding date knowing the Fort Bliss exercise would be complete well before that date, but unfortunately, real world things occur without concern for scheduled events, even a wedding. Our conversation ended with me telling Jason he would be able to call her once we were on the ground for a few days in Somalia. That was the best I could do.

Again, it is not easy being a leader, but doing the *hard right* thing is necessary, and Jason Coleman understood this. The happy ending to this story is that Jason and his bride Kim were married immediately upon our return to Fort Benning in late October 1993.

The soldiers of Task Force RANGER had approached the mission each and every day with great concern and vigilance regarding security. It is a real shame that others did not share similar concerns for the mission and the welfare of the Task Force. This compromise of security resulted in our loss of any surprise we may have had over the enemy, as well as significantly increasing our on-the-ground security requirements once in Mogadishu. Well, I did get off the plane with MAJ Stockwell and conduct the required media interview. I gave them a simple mission statement (without focusing on Aidid), a few comments on preparation of the force, and answered one question, which was related to the capture of Aidid per the UN General Resolution. I restated our simple mission statement that was as follows…

*When directed, Task Force RANGER deploys designated forces to Mogadishu, Somalia to reinforce the UNOSOM II Quick Reaction Force (QRF).*

I then said we would capture Aidid if we happened to see him in the streets. My interview was short and to the point, but some of my friends told me it was awful because I didn't say anything of real importance. To me that meant that the interview was a perfect success because I was able, without lying, to protect important information that could, in turn, protect the lives of my soldiers and innocent Somalis.

★   ★   ★   ★

Now that the interview had been handled, it was time to move on to business on the ground. It is important to note right up front that Task Force RANGER did not work for the United Nations force in Mogadishu; it was a separate entity and operated autonomously under the command of Major General Garrison. This does not mean there was no communication or coordination between the UN Headquarters there and Task Force RANGER; indeed it was constant and routine between these two elements. This interface was accomplished in many ways. First was the placing of two key people from Task Force RANGER with the UN Headquarters: COL John Vines of Task Force RANGER, who served as MG Garrison's liaison and was with the UN forces Deputy Commander, U.S. Army Major General Thomas Montgomery, nearly twenty-four hours a day, seven days a week.

The other key person placed within the UN Headquarters as a

liaison was Major Craig Nixon, one of my officers from 3rd Ranger Battalion. MAJ Nixon was placed with the 2-14th Infantry Battalion from the 10th Mountain Division as my liaison with them. This battalion was the UN forces Quick Reaction Force, the UN's most effective and professional combat-ready element. MAJ Nixon's liaison with the 10th Mountain Battalion Commander, LTC Bill David, enhanced the flow of information and facilitated better operational tactics and techniques awareness with these fighting forces.

Furthermore, there were regular meetings between key personnel from Task Force RANGER with key personnel from the UN Headquarters. MG Garrison and MG Montgomery talked almost daily either in person or by radio. My key personnel and I also had numerous face-to-face meetings with LTC David and his subordinates to discuss operational tactics and techniques. There were occasional joint training opportunities between my B Company and the companies of the 2-14th Infantry Battalion. The important type of training that occurred between the B Company Rangers and the 10th Mountain Division soldiers was focused specifically on three key areas: reinforcement operations by the QRF, clearing of buildings, and assistance with a possible downed helicopter. The training and interface between these units and the personnel proved to be enormously important on October 3–4, 1993, in the streets of Mogadishu.

★   ★   ★   ★

Even though Task Force RANGER did not work for the UN, the UN did have input into the living and operations location of the Task

Force. The location was an empty hangar at the airfield (our primary lodging area) which was adjacent to an empty, somewhat damaged concrete building (our operations building/headquarters). The hangar, the operations building, and the surrounding area were not prepared for us in any way by the UN prior to our arrival. Obviously, then, the first priority was to prepare our area.

Hangar, on the left, was the living area for Task Force RANGER. On the right side is the damaged concrete building that was the Operations Center.

The next requirement was to establish our compound and secure it. We did this by using our large metal equipment containers to build a wall that would encompass the hangar and operations building while providing enough area to protect our vehicles and Little Bird helicopters. Once this "wall" was set up the security positions were selected and prepared accordingly. A total of six security positions were designated that included an entry/exit point (with only one-way in or out) and five other positions that ensured complete security coverage. These six positions were manned twenty-four hours a day with two Rangers at each position. There were two

Entry/Exit Point

The Task Force area during the early stages of making it a secure compound.

A look at the guard shack that was built for the entry/exit point where two Rangers were in position at all times.

shifts in a twenty-four hour period, so now twenty-four Rangers were pulled from the primary mission to provide security. Even merely posting this modest number of soldiers to these positions made me, and other leaders, sorely miss the one hundred others who were not allowed to participate in Task Force RANGER. As a matter of fact, when the decision was made by MG Garrison to secure our area, it was evident that this would further reduce the force available for any mission. Therefore, a request was made by MG Garrison back to USSOCOM Headquarters for the forty-six man Ranger platoon that had been cut from the original deployment force. This request was disapproved. What a *stupid* decision that was!

The view out the back of the Operations Center building towards the city. It was too close (approximately 50 meters) to the city street and buildings for permanent security not to be in place—easily reachable by the enemy with AK-47s and RPGs.

On a few occasions, it has been argued that maybe the use of the twenty-four Rangers on security was unnecessary, and that their value on a mission was more important, especially on October 3–4, 1993. The answer to that is *yes* and *no*. There is no doubt about the fact that the Rangers would have been valuable on each and every mission; however, to say that value would have been greater than the necessity to provide security is not totally accurate. We had been told by the UN there was no need for us to be concerned about security because the UN force was providing security around the airfield perimeter. However, after a quick assessment of what was being provided by the UN force in the vicinity of our compound area, it was more evident that we did need to provide our own security.

For example, from the back side of our operations building it was approximately fifty meters to a main road that ran adjacent to the airfield—and on just the other side of the road were city buildings. A simple security assessment by the Task Force leadership concluded that this was a tremendous security risk because of the likely possibility of RPGs (rocket-propelled grenades) being fired from a position across the road or from a vehicular platform on the road. Furthermore, the closest UN security position to our specific area was a couple hundred meters in either direction along the airfield perimeter. This was totally unacceptable to the Task Force leadership.

This need to provide our own security was further emphasized from a historical perspective: the awful and painful memories associated with the events of Beirut, Lebanon (April 19, 1983) and Khobar Towers (June 25, 1996) will always remind us that security must be a primary focus for any US force on foreign soil. Both of these incidents exemplify two very important and basic requirements when the United States operates on foreign soil. First, the need to always ensure security for any US personnel and a related facility/building must be satisfied according to our standards and done by U.S. personnel. Second, we must constantly be aware of the danger of terrorism in the world and do everything possible to protect our nation and its people against this danger. The assessment by the Task Force clearly revealed that the UN provided security was not even reasonably adequate, especially around our compound area. Simply put: for the Task Force to successfully conduct operations and complete its mission, it must be intact from a personnel and equipment standpoint at all times—this meant having nothing less than perfect, sustained security.

The critical nature of this requirement can be best understood through an example of poor security measures by the UN along the airfield perimeter. Late one night, after the Task Force had been in Mogadishu about ten or twelve days, some shooting took place along the airfield perimeter about two hundred meters from our compound area. This did not sound normal because it seemed to be coming from one direction only and was not caused by two forces firing back and forth at each other. After some quick assessment, I was given the O.K. to send an element to check it out. This team of five Rangers with a Sergeant leading proceeded to "gear-up" with their equipment (full uniform with protective vests, night vision goggles, weapons, etc.) and move to the area. It took them about five minutes to "gear-up" and get to the area of concern—a security position occupied by three UN soldiers. It was being fired upon by an enemy element positioned near the road, but was not returning fire.

They were not returning fire *because they had no ammunition for their weapons*. They were trying to provide security without the ability to return fire.

The Ranger Sergeant immediately assessed the situation and returned fire at the enemy. The Sergeant and his five-man team were successful and the enemy probe was ended. Some of the enemy personnel were able to flee the area, but most were killed by the Rangers. By the way, the Ranger Sergeant did not radio me for permission to engage the enemy; he simply knew the rules of engagement and acted accordingly. He did, however, radio me after engaging the enemy.

This enemy action was most likely a probe made to find a weak spot in the airfield perimeter security so that a night attack could be mounted inside the airfield, which could have been devastatingly deadly. This activity was reported to the UN force leadership. The bottom line to security is this: it is absolutely necessary for the safety of the force, and best done to the correct standard, when you do it yourself. This particular security incident became an important point of interest during a session with the Commander-in-Chief and others in the Oval Office of the White House on November 11, 1993 (Veterans Day).

The Task Force compound area after it was "walled in" with metal containers with one entry/exit point only. The front of the hangar was covered with large metal vans. Sandbags were placed around key areas such as the MH-6 Little Bird helicopters for protection from any enemy mortars landing nearby.

*   *   *   *

More pre-combat preparation to be done involved routine physical training, marksmanship training with all assigned weapons, fast-roping and maintenance of all equipment (weapons, vehicles, helicopters, radios, night vision devices). These basic training routines were an important part of the soldiers staying focused and sharp for the combat mission at hand. They included 1) physical training involving weight training, the normal pushups/sit-ups, and a good run inside the airfield perimeter; 2) marksmanship training that was done on simple ranges prepared by the Task Force along the beach, or off helicopters for sniper personnel; 3) fast-rope training that was generally conducted as an element of the primary task of securing a downed helicopter, and 4) constant maintenance of all equipment. This was of critical importance because of the austere conditions in the hangar combined with the sandy environment, the high humidity, and the salty ocean air. As stated earlier, routine

Task Force personnel moving to helicopters to train. Training involved fast-roping or engaging targets with assigned weapons while flying.

It was common to encounter some of the local Somalis while out training.

training was essential to keep the Task Force personnel mentally as well as physically sharp on a daily basis. A letdown on any day was unacceptable because it could prove to be deadly.

One last piece of routine preparation that had to be considered was that of feeding the Task Force. Initially, for about the first eight to ten days, the food preparation was simple because it amounted to opening your choice of MRE (Meal Ready to Eat) and drinking your bottle of water. We did have cooks from 3rd Ranger Battalion, but there was no flow of real food coming into Mogadishu for us right away. This changed after about a week or so; then some real meals were prepared by the cooks. The normal day consisted of a hot breakfast meal, a MRE lunch, and a hot dinner meal, which was generally good (but never included prime rib or the like by any means!) While the two hot meals/one MRE was the norm an actual mission or some training could cause that to change, and did a few times. Personally speaking, I was very pleased with the food situation while there with one exception: the standard vegetables for every dinner meal for at least the first two weeks were peas and carrots, which are the only vegetables I did not ever like—and really hate now—especially the peas.

After meeting all these challenges, we were finally ready to execute combat operations.

# Operations Prior to October 3 | 9

The first of seven combat operations executed by Task Force RANGER in Mogadishu occurred in early September, and the final one was conducted on October 3–4, 1993. The basic operational template, as it is often called, was generally the same for all seven. There were two tactical operations conducted that were not focused directly on our stated mission of capturing Aidid, but were certainly indirectly related and important to accomplishment of the mission.

Soon after we were comfortable with our location and security at the airfield, it was decided that our presence should be made apparent to the Somalis, which meant it was time to be proactive and not just sit waiting for something to happen.

The decision made by the Task Force leadership was to conduct a daylight tactical reconnaissance of the city by vehicular convoy with air cover provided by the Task Force aviation element (Black Hawks and AHs). This was conducted also as a show-of-force to the Somalis, especially since they already knew we were sitting at the airfield. As the convoy of combat-ready HMMWVs moved through the streets of the city, the Somali people seemed surprised, even shocked, that these American soldiers had the audacity to do something like this, especially during broad daylight. Their reaction was exactly what we had hoped to create by doing this. In my opinion, it was saying to them that "we are here and will come out here whenever necessary to accomplish our mission"—capturing Aidid and others as necessary. This tactical operation was a success since it definitely caused a stir in the city and created the opportunity for future operations. It was also a great success in that no one fired a weapon; we were combat ready, but were not trying to create a situation of direct combat.

The second operation was executed because the Somalis were routinely firing three or four mortar rounds at the airfield with the rounds landing somewhere within its perimeter. There was little to no accuracy in the shooting; the Somalis were firing very hastily and did not produce any casualties or much damage to equipment. On one occasion, however, there was some minor damage to a few of our Black Hawk helicopters from one of these mortar rounds. It was clear that the potential for casualties and equipment damage definitely existed, and something had to be done to better protect the force. So the Task Force leadership decided to conduct nighttime combat patrols to capture or eliminate the mortar-firing Somalis. A Ranger Platoon was required to go into the city on foot to locate the Somali mortar-men. When the first platoon combat patrol was executed, it was done under my direct leadership as the senior person in the patrol. I must say the feeling during this operation was one of discomfort and caution. The platoon encountered minimal resistance during the operation with only one minor exchange of gunfire taking place, and that night no mortar rounds were fired at the airfield. The next night another platoon combat patrol was executed under the leadership of CPT Mike Steele, the Company Commander. There was so little resistance that we were able to pass out MREs to innocent Somalis in the streets.

The B Company Commander, CPT Mike Steele (right), and I inside the hangar where Task Force RANGER soldiers lived while in Somalia.

That night, again no mortar rounds. This was success, even though no Somalis were captured. Unfortunately the UN decided we were overstepping our mission requirements and told us to cease patrolling operations. With the first night of no patrols, there were numerous mortar rounds—probably six-to-eight fired at the airfield. Even though it was obvious that the patrol operations had hindered the Somali mortar firing, none were conducted again, not even by any UN elements, presumably because it was too dangerous for them.

As previously mentioned, a total of seven combat operations were conducted by the Task Force while deployed to Somalia. The first six of the seven operations were conducted based on reasonably sound intelligence provided by various sources. The intelligence gathering process in Mogadishu was very difficult for many reasons. Prior to MG Garrison's approval for a mission to be executed, a great effort was made by all concerned to confirm the accuracy of the intelligence regarding a respective target. Ideally any intelligence regarding a target should be one hundred percent confirmed; unfortunately that is not totally realistic. So often you are dealing with good but somewhat imperfect intelligence and are forced to prepare for an operation with contingencies in case things are not exactly what they seem to be.

*    *    *    *

Now I want to look at the highlights of a couple of the first six operations. The first was conducted in early September at the Lig Ligato Compound, which was thought to be a safe house for some of Aidid's fighting force. The intelligence regarding this compound turned out to be inaccurate, despite its confirmation by the UN intelligence staff prior to execution. The target was hit with great precision at around 2am, and personnel were captured and removed from the building. Unfortunately, the captured personnel were UN workers, not Somali fighters, but at least no one was injured.

There is, however, another little-known aspect of this operation that should be pointed out as a positive. The Task Force convoy of nine HMMWVs which I had moved to a support/holding position in the vicinity of K4 circle from which we could observe the

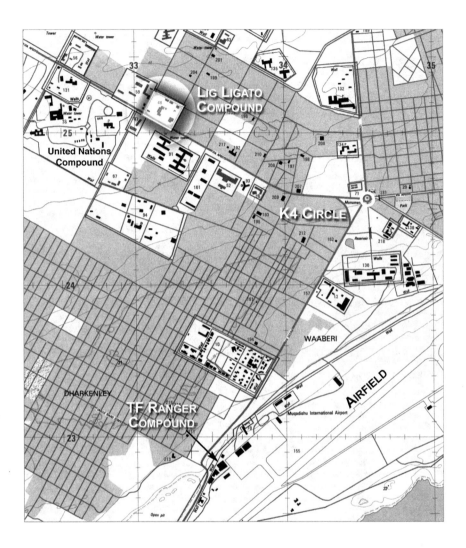

Lig Ligato Compound. During the operation, when personnel were actually fast-roping into the compound, we observed someone on top of the hotel just across from Lig Ligato. This in itself was uncomfortable and disturbing because we were unsure if this was just someone watching or if it was a Somali fighter preparing to shoot at our helicopters and personnel.

My order to the convoy personnel was to maintain 360-degree

security, but I also wanted two .50 caliber machineguns (5 HMMWVs mounted with them) and two MK-19 grenade launchers (4 HMMWVs mounted with them) aimed at the potential threat on the top of the hotel. I felt that one person was not a likely threat, but if more people appeared on the roof the threat became significantly higher. The next thing that occurred increased the threat immediately, and almost led me to order suppressive fire placed on that rooftop: the person on the roof placed something on his shoulder and aimed at Lig Ligato. Thinking that this could be a shoulder-fired weapon like an RPG, I immediately told the gunners on the two .50 cals and two MK-19s that were aimed at the rooftop to prepare to engage, but await my order to fire. I continued to observe this individual's actions using my night vision device and binoculars. After a few minutes of observation, I considered this person to be a non-threat due to the passiveness of his actions. I surmised that the shoulder-mounted device was a camera used by someone from the media pool in Mogadishu. This was exactly right: a cameraman was filming our actions at the Lig Ligato Compound—primarily the fast-rope insertion—and his piece appeared on U.S. television news in the following days.

This person was very lucky that night not to be killed. He presented a threat, plain and simple. The positive aspect is that there was no unnecessary action taken by the Rangers in the convoy. This exemplifies great discipline by every Ranger, as well as great control by every leader in the convoy, especially the non-commissioned officers. Also, it shows that there was no desire to just shoot and kill people. We were running a precise and controlled operation.

★   ★   ★   ★

The next significant tactical operation to occur was one that very nearly accomplished the primary mission of capturing Mohamed Farah Aidid. It focused on a group of buildings referred to as the Military Compound, a complex that served as the military's occupancy during the years when a legitimate Somali government was in existence.

The key intelligence received for this operation was that Aidid would be meeting with others in one of the buildings in this compound area. This intelligence was received on relatively short notice, but after an analysis of the Military Compound area, the recommendation to execute the operation was made by the Task Force leadership to MG Garrison, who gave his approval. There were multiple buildings in this compound area, but not so many as to make assaulting them impossible. This operation was executed superbly, in my opinion, even though Aidid was not captured that night. It was confirmed that Aidid had been in the compound area for a meeting, but had concluded it and hastily departed the area. Later information indicated that we had missed capturing him by mere minutes. He was now very scared of being captured and would most likely go into hiding to avoid capture, which is exactly what he did.

Now his four or five key leaders would have to execute all his orders without his physical presence in front of the Somali people. This in itself was a significant success for Task Force RANGER, and was a positive step toward accomplishing our mission. Prior to this operation, Aidid had been trying to make his presence known to the Somali people as often as possible and he would periodically hold a rally at a place known as the Reviewing Stand. This kind of open presence ceased soon after our arrival in Mogadishu.

The Reviewing Stand area was also an important part of the Military Compound undertaking. Upon initiation of the operation, the convoy of nine HMMWVs moved to a designated overwatch/support position that provided observation of the assault on the Military Compound and also placed us close enough to react very quickly if needed. This position placed us in the immediate vicinity of the Reviewing Stand. Some large gatherings had taken place there since our arrival, but none with Aidid in attendance. Our arrival at the Reviewing Stand overwatch position coincided perfectly with the assault on the Military Compound, done by fast-roping from helicopters and fire support from AH-6 Little Birds. About ten minutes after the convoy assumed its position we started receiving sporadic enemy fire, and after another ten minutes it increased significantly.

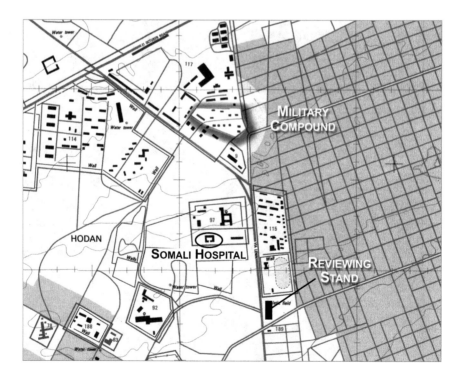

This was our first major confrontation with the enemy, and it came from two different directions, both from our front and rear. We mounted a counterattack with four of the gun-mounted HMMWVs (two .50 cals and two MK-19s) focused on the enemy fire from the rear, which was five hundred or six hundred meters from our position. The suppressive fire from these 4 HMMWVs and their personnel rapidly quelled the enemy fire from the rear. The major fight for the convoy personnel was to the front, in and around the Reviewing Stand area. To best fight this attack, I directed a dismounted attack by the personnel of the remaining five HMMWVs with supporting fire provided from the .50 Cals and MK-19s of those five HMMWVs. I chose to personally lead this dismounted counterattack, and so we went at the enemy.

In the meantime, we had reported this to the Operations Center and requested AH-6 support. Two AH-6s provided awesome fire support on the enemy, especially those we were unable to engage directly because of their location. Our dismounted counterattack was successful, and the enemy attack ended almost twenty minutes after its beginning. Not only was the enemy defeated, but our success was further exemplified by the fact that we sustained only two minor WIAs and no KIAs, while the enemy sustained heavy losses.

One of the two WIAs was the .50 cal gunner on my vehicle, SGT Mike Pringle. He is pictured with me on the front cover of this book with his machine gun. During this battle, SGT Pringle had received a grazing bullet wound to the side of his head, but never stopped engaging the enemy. I have been blessed to remain in contact with many of those who served in Task Force RANGER, most especially the Rangers of 3rd Battalion. Mike Pringle is one with whom I have remained in contact over the years since I left 3rd Ranger Battalion

SGT Mike Pringle, the .50 Cal gunner on my HMMWV. He was wounded during the Reviewing Stand battle—a grazing wound to his head just below the kevlar helmet.

in July 1994. As a matter of fact, he attended one of my speaking events in the Portland, Oregon area where he is a Lieutenant in the Portland Fire Department. The night before that speaking session I enjoyed dinner with Mike, and his wife and parents. During dinner conversation, I asked Mike's mom what her thoughts had been when she heard that he had been wounded. She said her immediate reaction was very concerned; however, when she was told it was a grazing wound to the head she felt better because that was always the "hardest head in the world." Aren't mothers wonderful?

Even though Aidid was not captured during the Military Compound operation, the final results were a success because, first and foremost, we had been close enough to capturing Aidid for him to change his personal manner of operation; thus, he was seen much less by the Somali people, and especially by his clan. We also captured some enemy personnel and killed many others while exhibiting our ability to fight them on their ground at night and win. And, very important indeed, our morale went from good to great, whereas theirs went from good to bad.

⋆   ⋆   ⋆   ⋆

The final operation to be highlighted took place on September 21st. By this time in September, the Task Force had expanded its mission: not only was it the capture of Aidid but also the capture of his key leader personnel as well. This had become important because Aidid had pretty much gone into hiding to avoid the possibility of being captured; we had scared him. He therefore was now directing things to happen through his key people, not by his personal presence.

On September 21, a very significant operation was executed which led to the capture of Osman Atto, as he was Aidid's right-hand man, as well as his arms dealer and chief financier.

This operation actually started out as a target building assault but became a vehicular convoy takedown. It was initiated in mid-morning and was based on intelligence information proved to be accurate, that Osman Atto would be meeting with others sometime that morning in his house. As the meeting was about to begin, we were standing by ready to execute the operation. A few minutes after everyone was in the house, the order was given by MG Garrison to execute, and with that the aircraft lifted off and the convoy departed the airfield. Within moments of our departure, the call came over the command radio net to halt the convoy and return to the airfield. What had happened was that Osman Atto and some of the others had come out of the house and departed in three different vehicles. This operation had now become a vehicular assault instead of a building assault, and as our convoy was not a principal part of a vehicular assault we would remain at the ready to move if needed.

The change from a building to vehicular operation was not difficult for the aircraft personnel, even though they were already airborne. Basically, it only required the helicopters to adjust positions slightly in order to have personnel where they needed to be to stop the vehicles, then capture the personnel. The necessary adjustments were made without any problem, and the vehicular assault was a success. It is important to note that the primary element for this action on the ground was the personnel from Delta Force. Also, the takedown was not as simple as walking up to the vehicles and taking Osman Atto and the others away without resistance. The vehicular personnel actually ran from their vehicles in an attempt to get away and engaged in a small firefight with the Task Force personnel; even Osman Atto attempted to escape the area.

All efforts to get away were futile. The key result was the capture of Osman Atto who was brought to the airfield by Task Force personnel. After brief questioning by Task Force leadership, he was turned over to the appropriate UN personnel for further questioning and imprisonment with other Somali National Alliance (SNA) captives, members of the Habr Gidr clan of Aidid. This was a tremendous success for Task Force RANGER and a significant blow to Aidid. He had just lost his right-hand man.

*   *   *   *

There were three other operations conducted, the results of which varied from limited success to no success at all. But it is important to note that no casualties occurred either, friendly or enemy. Also the civilian Somalis were friendly toward us and wanted peace returned to their streets. It was disturbing to see innocent Somalis being killed by their own people, and this could be a woman or a child who happened to be in the wrong place at the wrong time. Our concern for the health and welfare of the peaceful and friendly Somalis who were there in the streets of Mogadishu was never one of disregard or ambivalence. The personnel in Task Force RANGER did everything possible on every mission, including October 3–4, to avoid civilian casualties and collateral damage, and we were quite successful in doing this most of the time. This is a testament not only to Task Force RANGER, but to all members of the United States Armed Forces.

For example, there were occasions where medical care was given to Somalis while on an operation, and even at the airfield. Food was also provided to Somalis. This occurred while on operations; it may have only been MREs, but was certainly better for them than having nothing, especially the children. The American Soldier is truly a unique treasure—tough and dedicated as a defender of our nation, but kind to the less fortunate. I witnessed it in the most austere, toughest conditions possible, and it makes me proud to be called an American soldier.

# October 3-4...
# More Than a Battle | 10

In the words of Rick Atkinson, a friend and exceptional author, the battle of October 3–4, 1993 can best be described as "A tale of miscalculation, bad luck, and extraordinary personal valor by those in the fight…the most intense combat by U.S. infantrymen since Vietnam." Without question, the events associated with those two days could certainly be looked at in those terms. Many previous writings have provided reasonably accurate accounts of what occurred in the streets of Mogadishu on those days, which I have no desire to address or correct. I will, however, write about some of the things I was personally involved with.

Sunday, October 3rd, had started out like any other day in Mogadishu for us. There was physical training followed by personal hygiene time followed by a nice hot breakfast (eggs, grits, ham, bacon, etc). The entire Task Force then participated in the normal morning formation where we had our daily prayer, saluted our flag, and sang *God Bless America*, normally led by Colonel Boykin.

He was second in command to MG Garrison, and was essentially the operational commander on a daily basis. MG Garrison and COL Boykin formed one of the greatest command teams I was ever privileged to serve with in my career. The next important item on the schedule for that Sunday was the dinner meal, which was going to be steak—an unusual treat. So, as things were expected to go, October 3rd would simply be another day in Somalia for us—little did we know what was about to happen.

\*　\*　\*　\*

As the morning progressed all seemed to be normal and quiet for the Task Force, but around noon some intelligence was received about an important meeting that would possibly take place that afternoon. Around 1:00 pm the intel build-up regarding this meeting developed in such a manner that the possible meeting became a probable meeting; important details regarding the approximate time, general location, and possible attendees. Estimated time was believed to be around 3:00 pm; this gave the Task Force the unusual luxury of having two hours to prepare for a possible operation.

The general location was identified as a building near the Olympic Hotel, which was only a few blocks from the Bakara Market area, the most dangerous part of the city. When word came on the possible key attendees, this clearly became a top priority operation: Omar Salad, a Chief Advisor to Aidid, and Mohammed Awale, Aidid's Minister of Foreign Affairs. The capture of these two priority personnel, along with already captured Osman Atto, would mean that three of Aidid's key leadership personnel would be gone from the city. This would certainly cause Aidid and his organization much harm. It was even possible that Aidid himself would attend the meeting. This clearly was an operation of critical importance, but definitely the most difficult and dangerous one to date because it would be conducted in daylight and in the most dangerous part of the city.

The *go* for the operation was given by MG Garrison around 3:00 pm, but the Task Force would not launch from the airfield until the target building with attendees present was 100% confirmed by an intel source on the ground. Such confirmation was received at the Task Force Operations Center at approximately 3:30 pm.

*   *   *   *

The next event of great importance was hearing the codeword IRENE, which simply meant "execute the operation," the launch of the Task Force from the airfield, which occurred at 3:32 pm. The Task Force composition for this operation consisted of eight Black Hawk helicopters, four MH-6 Little Birds, four AH-6 Little Birds, some surveillance aircraft, and the vehicular convoy of nine HMMWVs and three five-ton trucks. Within minutes of transmission of the codeword IRENE over the radios, Task Force RANGER was on the move by ground and air to the target building.

The assault was about to take place, and the codeword LUCY would initiate it.

The movement of the convoy to the vicinity of the target was relatively smooth and uneventful; we received no enemy fire en route. The only unexpected development was a missed turn by the lead team of two HMMWVs under command of SSG Jeff Struecker. This caused no problem in that the third vehicle in the convoy, now

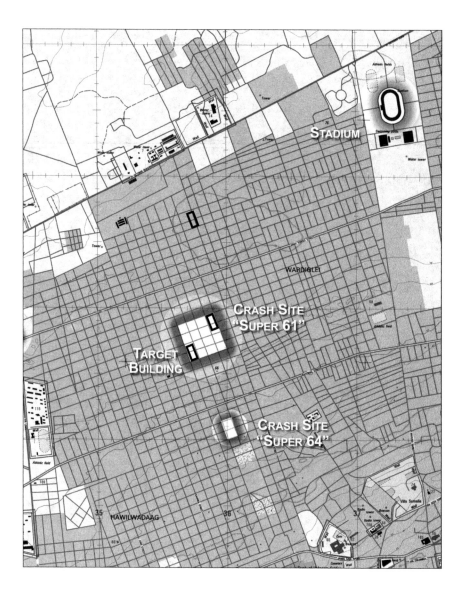

my command HMMWV, became the lead element and continued on the correct route. A few minutes after the convoy was in its holding position short of the target building, SSG Struecker's vehicles linked up with us. It is important to note that Somalia was not my first experience in preparing convoys for movement and leading them. As a mechanized company commander for twenty-two months in 1980–82, I had dealt routinely with tactical convoy operations. Although it was in training, not combat, the concepts for these types of convoy operations were similar and applicable. The air movement to the target area also seemed to be proceeding as planned.

\* \* \* \*

At approximately 3:40 pm, the codeword LUCY came across the radio to all element leaders and the assault was initiated at the target building near the Olympic Hotel. The convoy's holding position was some three or four hundred meters from the target building; therefore, I was actually able to observe the helicopter assault take place from a position near my vehicle. All seemed to be going fine. The assault by the Delta Force operators was swift, precise, and successful. During the time of the assault, the volume of enemy fire had increased significantly throughout the area. The convoy personnel had dismounted from the vehicles and were returning fire at the Somali enemy in every direction. Black smoke permeated the sky as the Somalis were burning tires at every intersection to summon their reinforcements to that area. In addition to being an effective technique for communication, the black smoke also caused visibility problems for the helicopters.

Things were really starting to heat up in the Mogadishu streets now. Within twenty to twenty-five minutes after the assault on the target, I received a radio call that the prisoners were secured and ready for pickup. I then moved forward to the target building with my vehicle only. I wanted to first make physical link-up with the

Delta element leader prior to moving the large convoy of vehicles into the open main road in order to minimize the time the vehicles would be most susceptible to RPGs. I immediately made face-to-face coordination with the Delta element leader, confirmed prisoners were ready for pickup, then called the convoy forward to conduct loading at the target building.

★   ★   ★   ★

As we were starting to load the prisoners, things changed very quickly. Ranger Todd Blackburn, who was just a few weeks shy of his nineteenth birthday, fell while fast-roping from one of the Black Hawk helicopters and plunged forty-five feet to the ground, landing in the middle of the dirt street. There are differing thoughts on what caused Ranger Blackburn to fall—he did not have a firm grasp of the rope; the large volume of enemy fire distracted him; a sudden movement of the helicopter caused him to lose control. I will say it was very unusual for someone to fall like this when fast-roping because Rangers conduct these operations on a regular basis, just like conducting airborne parachute operations. But it can happen and for some reason it did happen to Ranger Blackburn on this day; he sustained serious injuries and needed urgent medical care.

He received this life-saving medical attention while lying in this Mogadishu street; his friends were not about to let him die. The timely actions taken by Ranger Blackburn's element leader (SSG Matt Eversmann), three Task Force medics (Ranger medic Mark Good, Delta medics Kurt Schmid and Bart Bullock) and Ranger Sergeants Casey Joyce and Jeff McLaughlin were instrumental in saving his life.

SSG Matt Eversmann was an outstanding non-commissioned officer who had just assumed the leader role for this element of fifteen Rangers. The platoon sergeant, SSG(P) Chris Hardy, had departed for the States a few days prior because of the critical illness of his mother. SSG Eversmann was one of the very best Ranger squad leaders I had ever served with and was ready to assume this role. After Ranger Blackburn was stabilized as best as possible, he was placed on a litter and moved to my position at the target building. I asked Ranger Good what had happened and the extent of the injuries. He told me Ranger Blackburn had fallen off the rope during the insertion, and his injuries were very serious; he had a head injury, back injury, hip injury, and various internal injuries. Ranger Blackburn was unconscious and bleeding from the mouth, the nose and the ears.

Based on the medical recommendation, I quickly decided to conduct a casualty evacuation of Ranger Blackburn. I radioed the Operations Center to inform them of what was about to take place; the response was ROGER and that an AH-6 Little Bird would provide air cover during the evacuation. This had to be a vehicular evacuation as the enemy fire was far too intense to bring a helicopter down into the streets. I told SSG Jeff Struecker he would conduct the evacuation using his team of two gun HMMWV's with one cargo HMMWV (like a small open-bed truck). Ranger Blackburn would be placed in the back of the cargo HMMWV as the litter would slide in just like in an ambulance. As soon as the loading was complete, the small casualty evacuation convoy of three vehicles moved out with some Delta Force personnel in the cargo HMMWV to provide additional security and firepower to this small convoy. This unexpected incident had been dealt with and had not really caused anything to significantly change the primary operation of capturing the Somali enemy personnel at the target building.

\*   \*   \*   \*

As the loading of the prisoners at the target building was being completed, a second unexpected incident occurred that impacted the operation enormously—the crash of the first Black Hawk helicopter that day. Super Six One was hit by an RPG and was going down somewhere in the streets of Mogadishu. Super Six One had been hit in the tail rotor and the crash was uncontrolled and violent. The helicopter had crashed pretty much nose down somewhat on the pilot's side and did so in a relatively small alley after clipping the top of a building. This was a devastating crash that would result in casualties, both KIA and WIA. At the target building where the loading of the prisoners was being completed, I observed Super Six One spinning out of control on its way to the ground. It was evident we were about to have a change in the planned operation for that Sunday afternoon.

\*   \*   \*   \*

Meanwhile the three-vehicle casualty evacuation convoy was still making its way back to the airfield with Ranger Blackburn. A few enroute reports received from SSG Struecker made it very clear that the trip was no drive in the park. The small convoy had encountered heavy enemy contact with numerous roadblocks and firing from every direction imaginable. SSG Struecker had made sure that the vehicles kept moving because stopping would have been deadly.

Unfortunately, he had to report to me that the first KIA of the battle had occurred as the convoy was closing in on the airfield where it had encountered heavy enemy fire. Because standard operating procedure prohibits names of KIAs to be given over the radio, I didn't find out until I returned to the airfield later that the KIA was SGT Dominick Pilla, a great young man who had just been promoted to Sergeant after our arrival in Mogadishu.

SSG Struecker's three-vehicle convoy had successfully reached the airfield with Ranger Blackburn still alive. He was initially treated and stabilized at the airfield by the Delta Force Surgeon Major Rob Marsh and then evacuated to the field hospital. The medical treatment that he received from the medics in the streets to Doc Marsh at the airfield to the surgeons in the field hospital was truly incredible; they saved the life of this almost-nineteen-year-old soldier. Ranger Blackburn was among the very first casualties to be evacuated to Landstuhl, Germany for treatment at the Army hospital there. The next time I saw him was at Walter Reed Army Medical Center in Washington, DC after my return from Somalia in late October. He was on the road to a long recovery.

It is important to add a footnote about Todd Blackburn. As I stated earlier, I have remained in contact with many of those—of whom Todd is one—who served in Task Force RANGER, most especially my Rangers. He attended one of my speaking events; he was at my wedding in March 2006; and I was at his wedding in June 2006. Todd, Christina and their five kids live in Milton, Florida (his hometown) where Todd is a police officer in the Pensacola Police Department. Todd and Christina's youngest child is a boy named Dominick, whom they named after SGT Dominick Pilla—a living reminder that Rangers never, ever forget their Ranger buddies and their sacrifices.

\*   \*   \*   \*

Now that the first unexpected incident had been resolved it was time to focus on the handling of the prisoners and securing of Super Six One's crash site. Immediately upon word of the crash, the day's operation changed. No longer was it just the capture of some key enemy personnel, but it was also the rescue of the Task Force personnel in Super Six One: pilot CW4 Cliff Wolcott, pilot CW3 Donovan Briley, crew chief SSG Charlie Warren, crew chief SSG Ray Dowdy, and four Delta Force Snipers. At the target building the loading of all prisoners and Task Force personnel was complete and movement of the convoy was now possible. The immediate action by those Task Force personnel not loaded on the vehicles was to move to the Super Six One crash site by foot as quickly as possible. The convoy would move to the crash site as well and do so under directions from the Command and Control Black Hawk helicopter overhead—my command level counterparts for the Delta Force element (LTC Gary Harrell) and the Task Force 160th element (LTC Tom Matthews) were in that Command and Control Black Hawk.

The rescue plan was for all elements to move as quickly as possible to secure the crash site, then evacuate all personnel to the airfield by vehicles. The concept was simple and had been rehearsed, but execution was extremely difficult due to the large number of enemy personnel in the area and the constant heavy barrage of enemy fire, especially RPGs. Also alerted were the personnel from the 10th Mountain Division QRF battalion who became part of the rescue effort as well.

The crash site was secured rapidly by those Rangers and Delta Force personnel who were able to move by foot. As it turned out, this was a relatively small number as the fighting was extremely intense every inch of the way and movement for some was nearly impossible; others were held back by dealing with casualties. It was vitally important to secure the crash site rapidly in order to ensure that no personnel were captured by the Somali fighters, and this was accomplished at the Super Six One crash site.

*    *    *    *

Another very critical part of securing the Super Six One crash site was executed by the Combat Search and Rescue (CSAR) Black Hawk. The CSAR element was a routine part of every operation; however, it was one you hoped you never had to implement. On the previous six operations, the CSAR element had not been employed in any manner, but that would not be the case on this October day.

The CSAR Black Hawk helicopter was carrying fourteen personnel on board in addition to the two pilots and the two crew chiefs. These fourteen personnel included seven Rangers, five Delta operators and two Air Force PJs (parajumper medical personnel). The aircraft was under the control of pilot CW3 Dan Jollota when it arrived above the crash site. As it hovered to allow the fourteen CSAR personnel to fast-rope down, it came under heavy enemy fire. The last two personnel were going down the ropes when the aircraft took an RPG hit, an action that would normally result in the pilot immediately pulling out of the area. Dan started to pull out before realizing that there were two personnel still on the ropes, PJs Master Sergeant Scott Fales and Tech Sergeant Tim Wilkinson.

Under heavy enemy fire in a damaged aircraft, Dan Jollota held the Black Hawk in position so the PJs could get on the ground safely. His actions were critical to saving lives at the Super Six One crash site; had he not ensured that the two PJs reached the ground safely, Fales and Wilkinson's medical capability would not have been available to the injured personnel. Dan then managed to fly this damaged aircraft back to the safety of the airfield where he landed it with no crew injuries, even though the landing was a hard one. Dan Jollota exemplified a coolness and calm that few could ever imagine, much less have themselves. His aviator professionalism was a tribute to himself and to his unit, Task Force 160—the Night Stalkers.

Now the crash site was secured and medical personnel were on the ground. Unfortunately, medical resources were reduced fairly quickly as MSG Fales was wounded shortly after arriving. The burden of medical aid was now on the shoulders of TSgt Wilkinson. He shouldered this responsibility efficiently and without hesitation. There are more alive today because of the professionalism and commitment of Tim Wilkinson, a tribute to him and the other dedicated Air Force PJs.

*    *    *    *

Another extraordinary action that occurred early at the Super Six One crash site was that of the crew of the MH-6 Little Bird Star Four One, CW4 Keith Jones and CW3 Karl Maier. Keith and Karl had seen Super Six One going down and therefore knew where it had most likely crashed. After a quick search of the general area, they saw the crash site and proceeded to land close by.

This was an amazing feat by these two extraordinary pilots; they chose to land in an alley versus a larger open area to minimize

exposure to enemy fire. Their successful landing placed them relatively close to the downed Black Hawk and minimized enemy contact; however, the alley literally provided only inches of clearance
for the turning helicopter blades. CW4 Jones and CW3 Maier did
this in order to assist their fellow soldiers who were in the downed
Black Hawk. Their actions were significant in delaying the Somali
fighters from attacking and possibly overrunning the Super Six One
crash site. They also provided timely evacuation of the most seriously injured Delta Force operators, SFC Jim Smith and SSG Dan
Busch. Unfortunately, SSG Busch's wounds were so serious that he
died after being returned to the airfield on Star Four One.

Shortly after Jones and Maier had landed at the crash site, they
were joined by the first Ranger ground element to arrive from the
target building. This Ranger element, led by 1LT Tom Ditomasso,
had seen Super Six One when it was hit and on the way down. After
a quick report to his commander, CPT Mike Steele, 1LT Ditomasso
was given the *go* to move to the crash site. Tom's small element of
ten or so Rangers moved out quickly and arrived at the site of the
downed helicopter in a matter of eight to ten minutes. Upon arriving
they could see the mangled Super Six One Black Hawk, but could
also see the Star Four One Little Bird sitting in this little alley with
Karl Maier at the controls. After the departure of Star Four One,
1LT Ditomasso's element immediately secured the crash site along
with the CSAR personnel until other ground personnel arrived from
the target building.

A special note regarding Tom Ditomasso is most appropriate.
Tom was one of my Silver Star recipients for his actions that day,
especially at the crash site of Super Six One. He was a great young
leader then, and continued to lead in combat many times for over

twenty years in the Army; he retired after spending over ten years with SFOD-D. He and his wife Jodi served our country during some of its toughest times. He is one of my heroes.

⋆　⋆　⋆　⋆

The convoy had started its movement to the Super Six One crash site not too long after the Black Hawk had gone down. It now consisted of six HMMWVs and two five-ton trucks—three HMMWVs had been used in the evacuation of Ranger Blackburn and one five-ton truck had been disabled by an RPG hit upon arriving at the target building. Our new mission was to move to the crash site where all forces would consolidate; then we would load everyone in the vehicles including the personnel from Super Six One and return to our compound at the airfield. Of course, we still maintained our focus on the original operation of returning with the twenty-one captured enemy personnel as well. Even in the midst of the very challenging and somewhat unexpected situations that had already occurred, it seemed as though the day would come to an end in a relatively short time at this point. But the day still had more surprises, and they were not good ones.

⋆　⋆　⋆　⋆

Another action that had been rehearsed was the replacement of a Black Hawk if shot down during an operation. The downing of Super Six One meant the execution of this rehearsed replacement action was now necessary. Not too long after the CSAR aircraft Super Six Eight inserted its personnel at the Super Six One crash site, Super Six Four (piloted by CW3 Mike Durant and CW4 Ray Frank) was inbound to assume the orbit position previously occupied by the crashed helicopter. The orbit positions were important to the tactical execution as they provided a low overhead cover for the forces on the ground. After a few circular orbits had been completed by Super Six Four, it was hit with an RPG in the tail of the aircraft. At first it seemed fine, but then the aircraft started to spin out of control as the damaged tail came apart. It continued its spin to the ground and crashed hard. Fortunately, however, it landed flat, which meant that the crew of Mike Durant, Ray Frank, Bill Cleveland and Tommie Field all survived. The actions of the two pilots Durant and Frank during the fall from the sky were extraordinary. Super Six Four was on the ground and all personnel were alive, but they needed ground forces to arrive quickly before the Somalis overran the crash site. Help was needed desperately, but the Task Force was already stretched in every direction—where would it come from?

$$\star \quad \star \quad \star \quad \star$$

The 2nd Battalion, 14th Infantry of the 10th Mountain Division was the United Nations' Quick Reaction Force, and significant coordination and training sessions had taken place with them after our arrival in Mogadishu. The focus of these efforts had been to enable the QRF to be a reserve force that could reinforce Task Force RANGER if necessary—and that necessary time was now. Soon after the first helicopter crashed a QRF company under the command of LTC Bill David, the Battalion Commander, was dispatched from its location at the UN compound to the Task Force RANGER compound at the airfield; this QRF company had been alerted and was on standby since the operation started around 3:30 pm. Unfortunately, it had not been made fully aware of the seriousness of the situation and had moved to the airfield via the normal safe route around the perimeter of the city—a fifty to fifty-five minute trip versus the ten or twelve minute trip through the city to the airfield. After about twenty minutes had passed, the Task Force Operations Center realized the initial QRF company had taken the long route and would not arrive at the airfield for at least another thirty minutes; this was far too long to be able to provide the necessary assistance for the personnel at the Super Six Four crash site.

Another QRF company was immediately dispatched from the UN Compound with orders to proceed directly to the Super Six Four crash site. Prior to these orders the small convoy that evacuated Ranger Blackburn was ordered to move out to the Super Six Four crash site as quickly as possible. SSG Struecker's element of three vehicles with the non-wounded Rangers and Delta personnel who brought Ranger Blackburn back were refitted with water, night vision devices, IVs and ammunition and prepared to move out.

Other personnel who were not on the operation for various reasons, like the security detail at the Task Force compound, were crammed into any available space on the few vehicles that were not used on the initial move to the target area. At this point, there were an adequate number of personnel moving to the Super Six Four crash site, but it was unclear if they would get there fast enough to prevent more loss of life.

While all these reinforcing elements were attempting to move to the second crash site, the situation around Super Six Four had reached the point where the fear of the Somalis overrunning the area and killing or capturing the crew was nearing reality; ground forces were needed immediately. The movement of the Task Force RANGER reinforcing element from the compound was very slow and very hazardous because the Somalis had effectively prepared roadblocks with plenty of eager and lethally armed Somalis. The second QRF company had encountered similar difficulties in their movement and had been essentially stymied. Unfortunately it seemed that any assistance and rescue effort from either one of the elements was not imminent.

*    *    *    *

In the meantime, the main convoy under my command had been fighting through the streets inch-by-inch, foot-by-foot in an attempt to reach the site of the first helicopter crash. This was like trying to move through a gauntlet from hell. The convoy's movement was unbelievably difficult and even disjointed in many ways. Every street was cluttered with obstacles from damaged vehicles to tables and chairs to rubble from destroyed buildings; no clean, easy movement was possible. The difficulty of negotiating the streets was, of course, exacerbated by the extraordinary intensity of enemy fire which never lessened. It was also a situation that could not be avoided, simply due to the fact that the vehicles were easy targets as they moved slowly through the congested streets.

Indeed there were a few times when the convoy was actually brought to a halt. Either a vehicle was hit by an RPG or soldiers were severely wounded and needed immediate medical attention. When the convoy did halt, almost everyone had to dismount the vehicles and fight like they were at Custer's Last Stand. During any halt, I would try to move through the vehicles to assess casualties and vehicular damage, and to speak to my subordinate leaders. During one such halt, SFC Bob Gallagher, the convoy platoon sergeant, and I were discussing the next movements. As we were kneeling at the side of my vehicle, a hail of AK-47 bullets hit all around us and SFC Gallagher was hit in his left hand and arm. After pulling him closer to the HMMWV and seeing his wounds, my Air Force Combat Controller SSG Dan Schilling and I tended to him. The damage to SFC Gallagher's left hand was severe, so I removed his wedding ring and put it in my pocket. I did not want him to lose his finger if any swelling occurred. He was later medevaced to Landstuhl, Germany, then home to Fort Benning's Martin Army Hospital. I gave his wedding ring back to him after my return to Fort Benning in late October. Bob later gave me a card written with his wounded hand. He has continued to lead soldiers and has done so in numerous combat situations in Iraq, both as a Battalion CSM and a Brigade CSM.

Sir,

I can't find the right words to say thank you so I'll keep it simple. Your actions saved my life on 3 Oct 93 + I'm forever indebted to you.

RLTW
SFC G

P.S. A big thanks to Barbara for helping my family during this difficult time.

The convoy's directional movement was being controlled by the Command and Control Black Hawk of LTC Tom Matthews and LTC Gary Harrell. My commander counterparts were doing their very best to facilitate our movement with directions that were simple and avoided as much difficulty as possible. This was nearly impossible, however, because of the limited visibility caused by the black smoke that saturated the sky above the city. So the directions were given to me in a fairly timely and accurate manner and were based on what could be seen by the two LTCs sitting in a helicopter

My commander counterparts in the Task Force. To my immediate right is LTC Gary Harrell (SFOD-D) and to his right is LTC Tom Matthews (TF 160 SOAR). Gary and Tom operated from the Command and Control (C2) Black Hawk helicopter.

far above the city streets. Their vantage point was much different from mine, so I would sometimes not follow their direction to turn at a certain street or alley. This was because as I looked down a particular street or alley it did not seem passable even for the

HMMWVs, much less the larger trucks in the convoy. If I had turned as directed on a few occasions, the convoy would have reached a point where movement forward was impossible and the vehicles would have only been able to back out of the area in reverse. Furthermore, this lack of forward movement would have put us in a position to be attacked from all directions by the enemy; basically, we would have driven ourselves into an ambush, and that was something I refused to do.

The movement of the convoy through the Mogadishu streets was, therefore, disjointed and very difficult; high intensity combat causes that to happen. I was fortunate to have very good people with me in my command vehicle, specifically, my driver SPC Joe Harosky and Air Force SSG Dan Schilling. SPC Harosky, a young soldier in his very early twenties, was normally one of my radio operators; however, I handled the radios myself since we were moving in vehicles not by foot. I did have the necessary radios on me to maintain communications at all levels when moving around by foot. SSG Schilling was able to provide an additional communication capability that gave us the necessary redundancy for constant communications.

Joe Harosky drove our HMMWV—the lead vehicle, which is always subject to the first roadblocks, RPGs, hand grenades, and so on—through those streets on October 3 in conditions that were just indescribable. At times, he was driving with one hand while shooting out his window with the other one. Joe drove so well in fact that not one enemy round hit his side of the front windshield.

My side, however, was much different. Somehow my side of the windshield ended up with four distinct bullet holes. These rounds were what caused my neck and arm wounds. The HMMWV wind-

SPC Joe Harosky, the driver in my HMMWV. His driving ability on October 3rd was challenged beyond belief. He truly drove the vehicle to "hell" and back.

shield was ballistically very good but not bulletproof by any means; therefore, some rounds were deflected due to the firing distance and/or angle—thank goodness! The bullets that did penetrate the windshield caused serious shrapnel to hit me. Luckily for me, the dead center rounds that hit my windshield were deflected and did not penetrate; those that did penetrate the windshield were slightly off-center and did not strike me directly. The most likely reason my side was hit hard by enemy bullets versus the driver's side is pretty simple: the enemy knows that the front passenger seat of the lead vehicle is usually occupied by a leader.

Joe Harosky left the Army after his enlistment was over and went on to complete his civilian education with an undergraduate degree from Indiana University, Pennsylvania and a Master's Degree from the University of Pittsburgh. He pursued work in the area of international affairs for sometime before making a long-term career decision. I received a phone call from Joe one night; he wanted to discuss going back in the Army through the Officer Candidate School (OCS) program and become an officer. Due to his prior service and educational background, this was easy for him to do.

I gave him my advice, answered his questions, and provided him with a Letter of Recommendation. Joe Harosky completed OCS and became an Infantry Second Lieutenant. He went to Ranger School after completing his Infantry Officer Basic Course at Fort Benning. Lieutenant Harosky graduated from Ranger School with no problem in 2001; I attended his graduation at Fort Benning where I pinned one of my old Ranger Tabs on his shoulder. Joe's first assignment as an officer was in the 101st Airborne Division (Air Assault) as an infantry platoon leader where he participated in the first major battle after Sep 11, 2001—Operation Anaconda in Afghanistan. He later served as a platoon leader with 3rd Ranger Battalion, his old battalion from Somalia, while in combat in Iraq. Since Somalia in 1993, Joe has served in combat at least five or six times. He is now Major Joe Harosky serving in the Army's Special Forces branch. I am very proud of him.

After the convoy had meandered through the streets under my direction for well over a hour, I believed we were on the verge of becoming combat ineffective; we had suffered too many WIAs and KIAs and were almost out of ammunition. We had actually been very close to the Super Six One crash site during some of the movement, but were never able to see it and link up with ground forces in that area because of all the city buildings and so much black smoke in the sky. Additionally, some of the directions given were actually for the crash site of Super Six Four. There was an attempt made to have us move to that area to provide some much needed assistance, but this proved impossible as well.

The point had been reached where I felt the convoy would be more of a negative force than a positive one if we continued through the streets. It was also evident to me that many of the WIAs in the convoy needed immediate medical attention or they would become KIAs. My recommendation to the C2 element of LTC Matthews and LTC Harrell, as well as to the Operations Center, was to return to the airfield compound. Returning immediately would allow us to get rid of the prisoners and take care of our wounded, then rearm, refit, and return to the battle in better shape to provide the needed combat power. MG Garrison and COL Boykin in the Operations Center concurred with my recommendation and directed us to return to the airfield compound.

This was very difficult, knowing that many of our Task Force personnel were still fighting the battle in the streets. Upon getting the approval to return to the airfield, I decided to have one of my subordinate leaders take the position of lead vehicle. I wanted to be in the rear of the convoy to ensure that every vehicle and all personnel made it back in front of me; leading from the rear was not easy for me, but it was the right place for me at the time. One of the key leaders during the movement—along with some SEALs and Delta Force operators—was a young sergeant by the name of Aaron Weaver. SGT Weaver was near the front and really kept things together and moving. This convoy operation was not going to be easy—the Somalis felt they had us right where they wanted us and were not about to let us get out of the area without a serious fight every inch of the way.

\*  \*  \*  \*

While the vehicular convoys were encountering tremendous difficulty in their movements to the crash sites of Super Six One and Super Six Four, the situation at the two crash sites was significantly changing and vastly different. The Super Six One crash site had been secured by the ground forces from the target building and the CSAR element, but the one at Super Six Four was getting worse by the second. It was during this time that Super Six Two became directly involved at this crash site. Its personnel were pilots CW3 Mike Goffena and CPT Jim Yacone, crew chiefs SSG Mason Hall and SSG Paul Shannon, and Delta Operators MSG Gary Gordon, SFC Randy Shughart and SFC Brad Hallings. The Super Six Two personnel had observed the RPG hit Super Six Four and watched as it crashed. They had continued to observe and provide fire support from their orbit overhead as the situation at the crash site had become increasingly desperate. Because it seemed unlikely that any of the rescue convoys were going to get there in time, the personnel on Super Six Two felt compelled to take immediate action themselves. Clearly there was an urgent need to get somebody on the ground to provide security and medical attention for Durant and his crew. The Somali crowds were growing rapidly and moving closer and closer to the Super Six Four crash site. Without immediate assistance the crew would be overrun and Durant and his crew would certainly be captured or killed.

MSG Gordon and SFC Shughart felt they could do more if on the ground than in the air, and could provide medical assistance to any of the injured crew. The other Delta Operator SFC Hallings would remain on Super Six Two because he had assumed one of the gun positions when the crew chief was wounded earlier. SFC Hallings later lost his leg after getting hit by an RPG while manning the gun. This plan, however, was rejected by Matthews and Harrell in the C2 aircraft. Gary Gordon and Randy Shughart asked again to be put on the ground to help their fellow soldiers, and after some serious discussion between Matthews, Harrell and the Operations Center (MG Garrison and COL Boykin), Gary and Randy were given the green light to go in to assist the Super Six Four personnel. These two extraordinary men knew the dire situation that confronted them, but felt they could handle the situation until more help arrived. The pilots of Super Six Two, Goffena and Yacone, put them down in a somewhat open area, about fifty to seventy-five meters away. Gordon and Shughart made it to the crash site with little difficulty and immediately began taking care of the crew. They started with its pilot, Mike Durant by moving him from the aircraft to a small covered area behind the crash site.

The two Delta Operators returned to the aircraft to help others and found the Somalis attacking from all directions. Gary and Randy were now totally committed to a battle of survival as the Somalis came from everywhere and in overwhelming numbers. After a fierce but relatively short fight, the Somalis gained an advantage and overran the Super Six Four crash site. These two heroes gave their lives while trying to save the lives of their fellow comrades. Unfortunately, the only one to survive was Mike Durant, who was taken prisoner by Aidid's men. To say the actions of MSG Gary Gordon and SFC Randy Shughart were extraordinarily valorous would be an absolute understatement. These actions are the essence of what is truly meant by the words "I will never leave a fallen comrade to fall into the hands of the enemy."

\*   \*   \*   \*

During the time efforts were being focused on the situation at the Super Six Four crash site, the main convoy had been making its way toward the airfield compound. The convoy's movement was slow and deliberate in that most vehicles were significantly damaged and barely running. Some HMMWVs were moving on two or three flat tires and smoke was coming from almost every vehicle. One HMMWV was actually being pushed by the larger five-ton truck behind it. The movement was further slowed by the numerous roadblocks and the constant enemy fire that lasted until the convoy passed through the K-4 traffic circle area—the point of the convoy's last major fight. It was in the vicinity of this circle that the main convoy first encountered a rescue convoy of the 10th Mountain Division's QRF. This element was accompanied by some of the Ranger rescue HMMWVs led by Major Craig Nixon, my next ranking Ranger officer in the Task Force. Upon link up with these other vehicular elements, personnel were quickly moved to better vehicles since some of ours had totally quit operating and were destroyed in place. With the assistance of these other vehicles, the main convoy completed its return to the airfield compound, a most bittersweet arrival. We were at last able to turn over the prisoners to other personnel waiting for them. This part of the Sunday operation was now successfully completed—but there were still many soldiers who had not made it back yet. The bitterness turned to anger for me as I walked among those who had returned in the convoy. I was now able to really see for the first time the magnitude of the casualties we had suffered: there were far more WIAs than there were those with no wounds at all, plus, there were the KIAs. Even one would have been too many, but it was significantly more than one.

I moved among the greatest soldiers in the world, so many of whom were bleeding and in awful pain—Rangers, Delta Force Operators, SEALs, and others. I was urging the medical personnel, doctors, and nurses to do more faster. They already were doing everything possible and more, but I wanted it all done now. The medical situation facing the doctors and nurses was absolutely overwhelming; they were truly incredible in handling all the casualties. I then wanted to find those who had been killed in action—who they were and where they were now—and as I continued moving around the area, I found SGT Pilla, SGT Joyce, CPL Cavaco and Ranger Kowalewski—all KIA. I also found SGT Ruiz who was in very bad condition; he was evacuated quickly as he needed immediate surgery, but he did not make it. I also saw Delta Force Operator MSG Griz Martin who was critically wounded and later died from his wounds.

The final medical encounter for me during this time occurred when one of the doctors told me I needed my wounds taken care of, especially my neck wound which was dangerously close to the jugular vein. I told him, "Don't worry about taking care of me right now; you take care of all the soldiers first, I'll be fine." He consented but said that he would be back very soon; he was much nicer to me than I had been to him. I remember after I had seen all the wounded and killed that I walked away for a moment to my vehicle and beat it with my helmet in sheer anger. The convoy force had accomplished the mission of getting the prisoners back to the compound, but had been decimated, and beneath my deep sadness and pride was also a profound anger.

★   ★   ★   ★

Darkness was now falling upon the streets of Mogadishu and much of Task Force RANGER was still in the city. It was now time to commit all forces available to the Super Six One crash site, and to get every Task Force RANGER soldier back to the airfield compound as soon as possible. Unfortunately, there was no need to focus on the Super Six Four crash site since everyone there had been taken away, whether as prisoners or KIAs. All efforts were now focused on putting a force together to rescue the Task Force personnel who had surrounded the Super Six One crash site.

Darkness had brought some periodic calm to the fighting in the city streets, even around the Super Six One Blackhawk. The calm was occasionally interrupted when some Somali elements would try to attack the crash site, hoping to overrun it, but the Somali fighters were not very good in the dark, especially in comparison to our forces. Furthermore, the AH-6 Little Bird helicopters were as deadly at night as in day. When a Somali element would attempt an attack, the AH-6s would quickly quell it and destroy the enemy. A helicopter re-supply operation had also been conducted for the Super Six One crash site soon after the sun had gone down, bringing much-needed ammunition, food, water, medical items like IVs, and night vision devices.

The danger of this operation was very clear since two helicopters had already been shot down. The re-supply helicopter would fly rapidly into a pre-determined area where it would drop the carefully packaged items out of the aircraft from a height of roughly one hundred feet. The personnel on the aircraft would literally kick the items out. They would land in an area secured by the forces on the ground, who would gather them up quickly and move back to the buildings where the items would be distributed as needed. In addition to the ground forces securing the area, the AH-6 helicopters would provide cover for the re-supply helicopter; this operation was executed with great speed.

This re-supply operation was critically important to the well-being of the Task Force personnel there; it improved not only their fighting ability but also their staying power and their morale. Simply put, they were better prepared to continue the fight until the rescue effort could reach them. After some initial fighting, the situation around the Six One crash site remained secure and relatively stable through the night and early morning hours.

The decision made by MG Garrison regarding the rescue force was to use all possible assets from Task Force RANGER and the UN. After extensive coordination with the UN command, it was determined that the rescue force led by Task Force RANGER personnel would be supplemented by 10th Mountain Division QRF elements as well as by an armored element of twenty plus Malaysian armored personnel carriers and four Pakistani tanks. (No U.S. armored force was in Somalia.) After a fairly lengthy period of time, the rescue force was assembled and on the move just before midnight. The movement was relatively slow and deliberate because the rescue force encountered numerous roadblocks and received heavy enemy fire from the time it cleared the notorious K-4 circle area. At one point during the movement to the Six One crash site, an element led by Delta Force Operator SFC John Macejunas moved to the Super Six Four crash site to check for any signs of survivors, but there were none, only the signs of comrades lost in combat. What little could be salvaged from the crash site was picked up, and then the helicopter was destroyed by thermite grenades (explosive grenades of an incendiary nature). The destruction of the helicopter would ensure that nothing worthwhile, such as radios in the cockpit could be taken and used by the Somalis. The rest of the rescue force had continued to fight and move to the crash site of Super Six One. During these hours of darkness, the rescue convoy finally reached the forces surrounding the Six One crash site.

★　★　★　★

After a successful link up was conducted between the rescue convoy and the forces surrounding the Super Six One crash site, the loading of casualties was the first order of business. While the wounded were being loaded on the vehicles, efforts focused on removing everyone from the Super Six One Black Hawk helicopter, which was accomplished with relative ease in every case except that of pilot Cliff Wolcott. The difficulty encountered in removing him was due to the fact that he was pinned in the aircraft as it basically folded around him from every side on impact. Extricating Cliff presented an enormous challenge, but it would be done no matter what. Simply put, Cliff Wolcott was not going to be left behind—he was coming out with everyone else. After several hours of extremely arduous work, Cliff's body was removed from Super Six One. Now the rescue convoy was able to complete loading of all personnel and move out to Pakistani Stadium, a fairly safe area on the north side of the city.

During the loading, it became apparent that there was not enough room in the vehicles for everyone because of the large number of wounded personnel. Therefore, in order to get everyone out with the rescue convoy, numerous Task Force soldiers would need to ride on top of the Malaysian APCs. Because the Somalis had not stopped firing on the Task Force personnel around the Six One crash site,

the idea of riding on top of an APC was not very appealing to anyone. It was even less attractive since the hours of darkness were
gone and the rescue convoy would be moving to the Pakistani Stadium in broad daylight.

The decision was made to move by foot alongside the APCs until
the rescue convoy had cleared the area of possible heavy enemy
fire, then jump on the APCs for the continued movement to the stadium. This made sense and seemed like an easily executable action,
but unfortunately, it was not so easy. The coordinated movement of
the rescue convoy with the personnel on foot started out just fine,
with the rate of movement steady and deliberate. But when the lead
APCs cleared the congested city street area, they increased their
rate of movement and did so before the personnel moving alongside
the APCs could climb aboard. The foot soldiers had to start running
to keep up and even became separated for a period of time. During
their run, these men were subjected to sporadic enemy gunfire, but
nothing of any great intensity. These soldiers had to run maybe
one-half to three-quarters of a mile before reaching the Pakistani
Stadium safely. This most likely occurred because of a language
problem with the Malaysian APC drivers.

*   *   *   *

When the Task Force and 10th Mountain QRF personnel finally
reached the Pakistani Stadium, there was a great sense of relief that
this harrowing battle of almost eighteen hours had finally come to
an end. Many things were going on at the Stadium now that everyone
had closed-in: medical care for so many wounded, food and water
for everyone, evacuations of the most seriously wounded, and, of

course, accounting for everyone from Task Force RANGER. The only personnel not present were those associated with the Super Six Four crash site—Mike Durant, Ray Frank, Tommie Field, Bill Cleveland, Gary Gordon, and Randy Shughart. The question regarding these six men was whether they were KIAs or POWs, and that answer was soon to come.

Over the next couple of hours, Task Force RANGER personnel who were not evacuated to the field hospital for medical care were moved by helicopters or by vehicles along safe routes back to the Task Force compound at the airfield. By about 9:00 am on Monday morning, October 4th, Task Force personnel had cleared the Stadium and had either closed in at the airfield compound or had been evacuated for medical treatment. One of the most intense and epic battles in the history of the United States Armed Forces had come to an end—or almost to an end. The end would not be reached until the six members from the Super Six Four crash site were physically accounted for to our satisfaction. With that in mind, it was absolutely necessary to recover from this battle as quickly as possible because there may still have been a need to go find and recover our remaining six Task Force members on very short notice.

No one would be left behind, period.

# Aftermath and Redeployment Home | 11

The next operation would be to rescue the six personnel taken from the Super Six Four crash site—as a minimum bringing them back, but hopefully bringing them back alive. Refitting and rearming of the force was an urgent requirement since the opportunity to rescue our six comrades could occur on a moment's notice. One thing was certain: because of the considerable number of casualties, the force for a rescue operation would be much smaller than that on October 3, but regardless of its size, there would be no hesitation to conduct the operation if the situation presented itself. Unfortunately, the expected rescue operation never took place.

On October 5, the members of Task Force RANGER watched with horror the disturbing and atrocious images of American soldiers being dragged through the streets of Mogadishu. It was now obvious to everyone that the six personnel not accounted for from the Super Six Four crash site were most likely all dead. Not long after seeing this horrible TV footage, Task Force RANGER was informed that there was indeed one survivor—Mike Durant. This information came from the UN Headquarters which had received it from the Somali National Alliance (SNA) personnel. Thus, the KIA count had now increased by five whom the Somalis had brutally killed —CW4 Ray Frank, SSG Tommie Field, SSG Bill Cleveland, SFC Randy Shughart and MSG Gary Gordon. CW3 Mike Durant was now considered to be a POW, and his physical condition was not yet known. Mike's life had most likely been spared so Aidid could have a prisoner for negotiation purposes.

★   ★   ★   ★

Task Force RANGER now prepared for the rescue of CW3 Mike Durant. Additionally, it was imperative to find, recover and positively identify the bodies of the other five men taken from crash site and killed. Task Force RANGER would not depart Mogadishu until each and every member of the four hundred fifty person Task Force was physically accounted for and back with the rest. To ensure the success of any further operations, it was evident that the Task Force would need to be reconstituted by elements from the Ranger Battalion, SFOD-D and the 160th SOAR in the states. This request was made on October 4 and immediately approved; the respective units were notified and prepared for rapid deployment to Mogadishu.

These reinforcing elements would arrive late in the day on October 6. The units were A Company of 3rd Ranger Battalion, A Squadron of SFOD-D, as well as various assets from the 160th SOAR. It was over a period of the next seven days that the remains of these five KIAs would be recovered and positively identified. As it turned out, some identifications were only possible through DNA testing, not by physical characteristics. No question, however: the identification for each one was 100% positive. One of the most difficult things the element leaders, like myself, had to do was to go to the field morgue at the airfield and make a positive identification of their respective unit personnel who were killed in action; I did this for Rangers Joyce, Pilla, Ruiz, Cavaco, Smith and Kowalewski.

★   ★   ★   ★

Critical to be conducted as soon as possible was a simple memorial service for those killed in action to honor and show proper respect for the fallen members of Task Force RANGER. The memorial service in Mogadishu took place in the Task Force RANGER airfield compound area on October 6. It was a simple ceremony—brief, sincere, and heartfelt.

Our fellow KIA Task Force members would be honored and laid to rest back home before our redeployment took place. After the return of Task Force RANGER to the states, there would be a final memorial service at the home station for each respective unit, at Fort Benning (3rd Ranger Battalion), Fort Bragg (SFOD-D), and Fort Campbell (160th SOAR). Each of these units had significant representation at the other units' memorial service. After our service at Fort Benning, I, along with a few of my key leaders, attended those at Fort Bragg and Fort Campbell. The sense of that final closure was now reached, at least as much as humanly possible.

Later on the day of the memorial service in Mogadishu the reinforcing units would start arriving in Somalia. On this evening, just about dark, the Somalis conducted one of their mortar attacks—the first one since the October 3–4 battle. The normal three or four rounds were fired at the airfield, but in this case one of the rounds was devastating to Task Force RANGER. It landed in our compound area where numerous people were standing and talking. One was killed and quite a few were wounded, some seriously. SFC Matt Rierson, a Delta Force Operator, was killed instantly as the mortar round landed only a few feet from where he was standing. Matt had survived the intense battle of October 3 as part of the main convoy during the difficult movement through the city streets. He was instrumental in the convoy's fight and survival on that day; to have fought and led so magnificently in that battle and then to die so unexpectedly was not fair or right. Unfortunately, there is nothing fair about being in combat; there never has been and never will be.

MAJ Rob Marsh, the SFOD-D Surgeon. Doc Marsh was incredible in his handling of the casualties at the airfield compound on October 3rd when the convoy returned with the prisoners and so many wounded soldiers. He was seriously wounded when the mortar round landed in our compound.

Some of the others wounded from the mortar round included COL Boykin, LTC Harrell and MAJ (Doc) Marsh. The most seriously wounded were Harrell and Marsh, whose injuries were so severe that they almost died right there at the airfield. They were evacuated to the Landstuhl, Germany Hospital the next day. It is an understatement to say that this was devastating to the Task Force. A memorial service earlier in the day had brought some closure to the deaths suffered by Task Force RANGER on October 3, and now there was the need to memorialize one more. This was a mental and emotional challenge for everyone, but the Task Force came together, maybe closer than ever, and prepared for the next battle.

*  *  *  *

Next on our critically important agenda was to prepare the reinforcing units for combat in the streets of Mogadishu. After only a few hours on the ground in Somalia, they had witnessed the death and destruction of combat and realized its ugliness. The focus for me was to prepare my A Company Rangers for the next combat operation to surface, whenever and whatever it might be. B Company was not combat ready because of its loss of personnel at all levels; therefore, A Company would take the lead with augmentation provided by those B Company Rangers who were still combat effective. This arrangement afforded us an advantage in that our fighting force had increased in size and capability. The same situation applied to the SFOD-D Squadrons now on the ground. A Squadron would lead and C Squadron would augment. The 160th SOAR elements worked to replace crews and helicopters as quickly as possible.

Very simply, Task Force RANGER was going to be combat ready very quickly to complete the mission of capturing Aidid. His forces had now been dealt a devastating blow; two key leaders had been captured along with nineteen others, close to five hundred of his fighters had died, and over six hundred had been wounded—now was the time to finish the mission.

As it turned out, while we were reconstituting and preparing for the next operation, especially the capture of Aidid, former U.S. Ambassador to Somalia Robert Oakley was in Mogadishu negotiating with Aidid's clan leaders for the release of Mike Durant and the end of mission for Task Force RANGER. The Clinton Administration had already made the *easy wrong* decision, to turn and walk away from completing the mission—a big mistake. After a few days of negotiations Oakley secured the release of Mike Durant, but, as is the case with such transactions, the enemy made its own stipulation: there were to be no more operations to capture Aidid and our Task Force was to leave Mogadishu.

Naturally, this stipulation was easy for Oakley to concur with because the Clinton Administration had already acquiesced to this on its own. Thankfully, Mike Durant had survived his eleven days as a prisoner, and on October 15 he was welcomed back to the Task Force RANGER compound at the airfield. He was there long enough to get the cheers and HOOAHs he so richly deserved and then, after the singing of "God Bless America," he was placed on the plane, on his stretcher, for the flight to Germany and Landstuhl Hospital. It was a great moment for Task Force RANGER.

$$\star \quad \star \quad \star \quad \star$$

After Mike Durant's return and departure to Germany, we thought that it was time for the reconstituted Task Force to pursue completion of the mission. It was, however, within the next twenty-four hours that the Task Force was briefed on the pertinent details of Oakley's negotiations with Aidid. We were informed that Task Force RANGER was not to conduct any further offensive operations to capture Mohamed Farah Aidid or anyone in his Habr Gidr clan. Our GOTHIC SERPENT mission had been prematurely ended by the decision-makers of the Clinton Administration. We were to maintain our security posture at the airfield compound in order to defend ourselves only. The next operation to be planned and conducted now was the redeployment of Task Force RANGER back to the United States.

To a man, every member of Task Force RANGER was angry with this decision. We had gained the upper hand in this Somali situation after the horrific battle of October 3–4, and to back away now was wrong. Aidid's real fighting force had been devastated during the fight in the streets of Mogadishu on those two days, so capturing him was more within our reach than ever. We had gained a tremendous advantage militarily and mission accomplishment was imminent. Furthermore, to leave Mogadishu like this was totally disrespectful to the courageous American soldiers who had fought so hard there, to the nearly one hundred WIAs, and especially to those who had given their all and made the ultimate sacrifice: the seventeen KIAs of Task Force RANGER and the two KIAs of the 10th Mountain Division's 2–14th Infantry Battalion (QRF).

The negotiations by the Clinton Administration through Robert Oakley had brought the mission in Somalia to an abrupt and wrong conclusion. When negotiations are conducted with less than honorable people, such as the terroristic thugs of Aidid and his Habr Gidr clan, the repercussions will haunt you somewhere, sometime. A very simple but clear example of the negative impacts associated with these types of negotiations were the signs of weakness that were perceived by terroristic leaders such as Osama bin Laden and Saddam Hussein. Osama bin Laden used this sign of the United States' unwillingness to complete the mission to rally his terrorist forces. It was discovered that Saddam Hussein had shown a bootleg copy of the movie "Black Hawk Down" to his Republican Guard Army so they could see what he believed to be America's weakness to fight the fight to the bitter end. Both of them made a significant error, though; they failed to realize we would change Presidents in January 2001.

A warm welcome awaited the returning element of B Company to Fort Benning, GA. The element was smaller due to the number of KIAs and WIAs not present, about 60% of what had initially deployed.

All was said and done regarding Task Force RANGER operations in Mogadishu, and the redeployment of the Task Force would take place in the coming weeks beginning on October 25, 1993 with the redeployment of the elements of B Company, 3rd Ranger Battalion heading home to Fort Benning, Georgia. I led the first redeploying element. The units' arrival at Fort Benning's Lawson Army Airfield more than a day later was bittersweet to the returning Rangers. Everyone was happy to be home with family and friends cheering their arrival, but far too many who had deployed to Somalia in August were not part of the joyful return. Many were being treated in hospitals for the wounds they had suffered in the October 3–4 battle. There were also those who would never return to their loved ones at home because of their ultimate sacrifice on the field of battle. Within the next week, the remaining members of Task Force RANGER would redeploy to their respective home station at Fort Bragg, NC, Fort Campbell, KY or Fort Benning, GA. Task Force RANGER had reached "end of mission."

# Final Thoughts | 12

An important political aspect of the mission was associated with the adversarial relationship between the UN Secretary General Boutros Boutros-Ghali and Mohamed Farah Aidid; they had been serious enemies for quite some time. The UN Secretary General hated Aidid's Habr Gidr clan as well. Clearly, this mission's success would be very pleasing to Boutros-Ghali as it would remove Aidid and his clan from a position of power in Somalia—truly an example of politics at its worst.

It was also interesting that Aidid had a son, Hussein, who was in the U.S. Marine Corps, a little-known fact until the arrival of the Marines in Mogadishu in December 1992. His son was a U.S. Marine by virtue of his California mother, and he actually deployed to Somalia with the Marines in December 1992, but was not allowed to go ashore. In talking with some Marines since 1993, I have been led to believe that Hussein was a good Marine. He returned to Somalia after leaving the Marine Corps and was in Mogadishu in

August 1996 when Aidid was killed during clan fighting. Hussein has not been a major player in the goings-on in Somalia since his return there.

Not only did we encounter large numbers of Somali fighters on October 3–4, but we were also confronting an enemy of drug addicts. The drug of choice was a leafy one called *khat*, a mild amphetamine that had to be chewed for its effect. The *khat* chewing normally began in the late morning to early afternoon period; therefore, by late afternoon the *using* Somalis were jacked-up, aggressive and ready to fight. The *khat* high would last into the late evening; then the crash would occur. Thus, to conduct an operation during the middle of the afternoon, as happened on October 3, was not the ideal choice; late night was preferable. Unfortunately, when a target presents itself you must go, especially a high priority target as was the case on October 3–4, 1993. It is very interesting that *khat* has become a part of the U.S. drug problem today. There are some states, like New York and Minnesota, that have a significant Somali population, and *khat* is part of the drug war there.

*   *   *   *

Now for a few final simple but important clarifications. First, there were two McKnights in Task Force RANGER, not just one. They were Danny (Ranger Battalion Commander) and Dave (MG Garrison's staff intelligence officer). At the time, Dave was actually a Colonel, and I was a Lieutenant Colonel. We became very good friends during our time in Somalia, but my friend has since passed away.

Next, it is a simple fact that there was no "lost" convoy in the streets of Mogadishu on October 3. I believe this misperception may have been presented by many in the convoy because it seemed so to them, and that is understandable. That is probably because the planned route of movement changed after Super Six One was shot down in the city. The new route was created on the move with no time to stop and brief everyone in the convoy on the new movement plan. The key leaders in the vehicles were informed of the movement change caused by the crash. All of this I know to be correct because I was the leader of the convoy and in the first vehicle throughout the movement toward the Super Six One crash site. As previously discussed, the convoy's movement was very difficult for many reasons, but it was not "lost". I was able to know the convoy's general location at all times by virtue of the fact that I always had a point of reference during movement—the target building area near the Olympic Hotel.

Also, regarding my role in taking the rescue convoy back out to the Super Six One crash site during the night-early morning on October 3–4; I did not go out with the rescue convoy. My boss, COL Boykin, made the decision that I would not go, although I was prepared to move out when I received the order. COL Boykin said that there was enough senior leadership going already, and furthermore I was in no physical condition to go because of my wounds. I did not like his decision, or even agree with it, but it was not open for discussion.

The final clarification is of great importance to me personally and professionally. This point regards the perception that there was something of a poor relationship between Rangers and the members of SFOD-D, primarily negative from the Delta Force perspective toward Rangers. This is without question wrong in terms of the big picture. It may be somewhat correct relating to some very specific situations, but by no means correct in the normal day-to-day environment. From the viewpoint of Rangers, from me down to the very youngest Ranger, there was nothing but the greatest respect and admiration for the members of SFOD-D. They are the best in the world at doing the things they are called on to do, with our Navy SEALs right there next to them.

The incorrectness of this perception is further negated by looking at the historical make-up of SFOD-D. Most of its leadership had a Ranger unit background at some level, and most of the Delta Force Operators had come from a Ranger unit background as well. Many of the Task Force RANGER SFOD-D personnel had Ranger unit experience: consider COL Boykin, LTC Harrell, CPT Miller, MSG Gordon, SFC Shughart and SFC Hooten. Furthermore, numerous Rangers from Task Force RANGER's B Company would become members of SFOD-D in the years following 1993. So, if this negative perception is not justified, where did it come from? Unfortunately, the opinions of one or two individuals can sometimes become reality, especially when these opinions are considered to be contradictory to the expected norm. I believe the opinion of a member from the SFOD-D element in Task Force RANGER was its primary source; that individual was primarily responsible and possibly supported by another, but that certainly does not reflect the general feelings that were prevalent among the elements of Task Force RANGER. By no means do I think every Ranger did everything perfectly during those very, very tough days in October 1993, but that also applies to every member of the Task Force involved in the fight, including myself. To sum up, Rangers and SFOD-D personnel got along just fine with one another, and there will always be great mutual respect.

\* \* \* \*

It is extremely important to look at the impacts of some specific decisions made at the highest levels regarding Task Force RANGER and its mission in Somalia. It is equally important to look at those impacts associated with the final outcome of the events in Somalia, especially from the October 3–4 operation.

Much has been written and discussed about the lack of any U.S. armor forces on the ground in Somalia, as well as the possible impact on the October 3–4 battle. First, the disapproved request made for U.S. armor forces was not made by the Task Force RANGER Commander, MG Garrison, but by MG Thomas Montgomery, Deputy Commander of the UN forces in Somalia. It had been made in September, but was disapproved by the Clinton Administration, most likely by the Secretary of Defense. An armor force in Mogadishu would not have been a primary part of our plans to conduct an operation because our operational tactics focus on surprise, speed of action and violence of action at the target. But I do believe our operational planning would have included the armor force as part of any reinforcement action had such a U.S. element been on the ground in Mogadishu. Furthermore, I believe that the impact of no U.S. armor element being available on October 3–4 was minimal. Most of the KIAs occurred within the first few hours of the battle— so early, in fact, that an armor force would not likely have been employed as support by that time. I feel a U.S. armor force would have been most beneficial in the rescue effort of the forces which secured the Super Six One crash site; a reinforcement plan that included them would have facilitated the speed and efficiency of this effort simply because U.S. forces would have been supporting U.S. forces instead of Malaysian or Pakistani troops. Yes, there was some impact from the lack of U.S. armor force in Somalia, but it was not significant.

But I wholeheartedly believe that reducing the fighting force to four hundred fifty personnel and eliminating the AC-130 had the most significant impact on the Task Force, especially on October 3–4. These decisions were truly *stupid* and obviously made in an attempt to be politically correct and show political control by the Clinton Administration. All you have to do is simply look at how important the A Company platoon of forty-six Rangers could have been in getting to and securing the crash site of Super Six Four. The lives of Ray Frank, Bill Cleveland, Tommie Field, Gary Gordon and Randy Shughart could have been saved. These Rangers could have been inserted by landing near the crash site as MSG Gordon and SFC Shughart did, or could have fast-roped in soon after the crash. Unfortunately, they were cut from the initial training and ready force for a *stupid* reason—the appearance of a build-up similar to Vietnam. The difference between five hundred fifty and four hundred fifty will likely seem negligible to most, but not to the force on the ground in combat. The decision to reduce the force should not have been made, period.

The reduction decision would have most likely been mitigated had the AC-130 been available to support the operation, but another *stupid* decision had been made to eliminate it from the Task Force RANGER assets as well. This politically correct decision was supposedly based on the concern for collateral damage, which is always a military concern, but a reality that may occasionally occur in combat. The leadership within Task Force RANGER felt that the need for the AC-130 was not likely to occur on every operation, but if it did occur a serious situation existed. The AC-130 needed to be available. Yes, that serious situation *did* occur in the streets of Mogadishu on those October days, but no AC-130 was there to meet this serious need for fire support. The use of an AC-130 in special operations is generally considered to be surgical in many ways... the target focus for the AC-130 would normally be very defined, not just firing at an area on the ground. This target focus would ensure the safety of the U.S. forces while also eliminating the enemy threat and minimizing collateral damage; this was realistically doable for the AC-130 and its professional crew members. I had personally witnessed such professional action during combat operations in Panama in December 1989—Operation JUST CAUSE. Look again at the serious situation that existed at the Super Six Four crash site on October 3–4. I truly believe my five brothers-in-arms would be alive today had the AC-130 been available to provide some much needed fire support around the crash site. I think Gary Gordon and Randy Shughart would have been able to render medical aid and provide the needed close-in security while the AC-130 kept the enemy from massing and overrunning the Six Four crash site. The AC-130 would also have been able to support the QRF forces attempting to reach the site. It was also a known fact that the Somalis were scared to death of the AC-130 when it was flying above the city; they had shown a reluctance in the past to even walk in the streets and had nothing capable of shooting at it. Furthermore, the absence of the AC-130 left only one reasonable option for an overhead-cover platform during operations, and that was the Black Hawk helicopters. Yes, the employment of an AC-130 gunship could have kept the Black Hawk helicopters out of the immediate operational target area, therefore reducing the possibility of an RPG

taking a Black Hawk down. It is ridiculous and shameful that decisions based on supposed political correctness can cause American
soldiers to die unnecessarily. The *hard right* decisions, whether politically correct or not must be made to ensure mission accomplishment while taking care of our most treasured national security
asset—the American soldier.

★    ★    ★    ★

There were also some very significant impacts related to the final
outcome of the mission in Somalia and specifically to the events of
the October 3–4 operation. The results of the battle in the Mogadishu streets were devastating for both the U.S. forces and the
Somali fighters: the American casualties were eighteen KIAs and
close to a hundred WIAs, while the Somali casualties were close to
five hundred killed and over six hundred wounded. The importance
of these numbers was never realized from an operational perspective. The reality of the situation in Mogadishu had changed after the
October 3–4 battle; Aidid's real fighting force had been decimated
and he knew it. Now there was an opportunity to push extra hard
for his capture, particularly because he was without two additional
key leaders who had been captured that day. This opportunity, however, was never pursued. The political decision was made to negotiate and withdraw from Somalia without completing the mission.

This decision was so wrong for many reasons. First, it was totally disrespectful to the members of Task Force RANGER as well
as the soldiers of the 10th Mountain Division's 2nd Battalion, 14th
Infantry. The men from these units had fought for their lives for
almost twenty-four hours and had come away beat-up but not beat-

down. These American warriors wanted to complete the mission in Somalia, but were not allowed to do so; the next operation to capture Aidid never took place.

The next operation for Task Force RANGER was its return to the states. The disrespect of this decision was felt deeply by every member of the Task Force. Even more wounding was the disrespect to the memory of the 19 brave American soldiers who had made the ultimate sacrifice in Somalia and to their family members. It implied that the mission was not important enough to stay and complete. But it was important enough to finish and should have been finished. If it was not considered important enough to finish, then it should not have been started in the first place. Putting American soldiers in harm's way should never be done without total conviction and commitment to succeed in the end—failure to complete the mission is not an option.

The Clinton Administration's decision to negotiate and withdraw from Somalia was a sign of weakness by the United States; we sent the rest of the world a message that we fear the tough fight. No matter how you kill us, maim us, drag us through the mud, we will always negotiate because we are afraid.

The perception of weakness was further supported by two more decisions that led to extremely questionable actions by the Clinton Administration. Within a week or so after Task Force RANGER's return from Mogadishu, Mohamed Farah Aidid would attend peace negotiations and do so with an escort element of U.S. Marines— another slap-in-the-face to Task Force RANGER. Even worse: no peace was achieved in those negotiations or afterwards.

But the ultimate act of disrespect toward the men of Task Force RANGER occurred in late November 1993. The Clinton Administration once again went the way of political correctness—succumbing to the temptation to make the *easy-wrong* decision—and ordered that all the prisoners captured by Task Force RANGER were to be released and returned to their homes in Mogadishu. In other words, the achievements of Task Force RANGER's mission in Somalia were effectively erased by the Clinton Administration.

These signs of weakness would come back to haunt America in the future. A vicious man by the name of Osama bin Laden once said something like this: look at the Americans in Somalia, kill them, drag their bodies through the streets and they will run because they are weak. Osama bin Laden thus inspired his Al-Qaida terrorists to attack the United States of America on September 11, 2001. Much to his surprise, he found that the United States of America was not weak. There was no running from this attack; instead, the Bush Administration decision was to seek out the perpetrators of this act of terrorism and bring them to justice.[3]

As of this writing, our military forces are still on the attack, showing our strength and resolve to complete the mission that will, in the end, further enhance our security while protecting the privileges and freedoms of the United States of America—the greatest country in the world; it's not perfect by any means, but it's way ahead of whatever's second.

★    ★    ★    ★

Now for a brief look at another important but much disregarded part of the 1993 fight in the streets of Mogadishu by Task Force RANGER. This connects the association of terrorism to the Mogadishu events in that August-October 1993 period. In the early nineties, Osama bin Laden was supported by the Sudanese government and Arab community, and the radicalization process of the horn of Africa was well on its way. (Somali Islamic courts link with Al-Qaida.) Furthermore, a commonly known fact was that in 1993 a major training base for terrorists with links to Osama bin Laden was located in Sudan. The close proximity of Sudan to Somalia made it relatively easy for Mohamed Farah Aidid to receive some support from his "friend" Osama bin Laden; they both wanted to kill Americans. This was most evident in some of the Somali fighters' tactics. It was obvious that some of the Somali fighting force had been trained to fight together, not just individually or as part of a mob. Additionally, the use of RPGs to bring helicopters down was not a Somali tactic, but one learned from training in a place like the Sudanese terrorists' training camps of Osama bin Laden. Yes, we in Task Force RANGER were fighting terrorism in the streets of Mogadishu in 1993.

Another surprising association of Somalia and Task Force RANGER would come from the regime of Saddam Hussein. Based on Iraqi intelligence documents obtained by CNSNews.com and information subsequently revealed on October 4, 2004, there clearly were efforts made by Saddam Hussein to target Americans through the support of terror organizations like Al-Qaida. One memo specifically cites an order from Saddam to support attacks on Americans in Somalia. This memo was written in January 1993—approximately nine months before the Task Force RANGER battle in Mogadishu on October 3–4. It's reasonable to say that Task Force RANGER encountered more than just a ragtag Somali militia of clansmen when fighting in the streets of Mogadishu in 1993; we were, in effect, battling the earliest versions of Al-Qaida forces.

*   *   *   *

Finally, the truly bad and *stupid* decisions made by the Clinton Administration regarding the mission of Task Force RANGER in Somalia had far reaching impacts, some of which were felt for many years after 1993. It is clear to me that decisions based on political correctness equal the *easy wrong* decision, and the results are far too often devastatingly awful (failure). Conversely, the willingness to make the *hard right* decision will normally result in success; however, it may quite often require the leader/decision-maker to be politically incorrect.

I will close by simply saying *God Bless America.*

# Observations and Reflections | 13

Look at the events of 2009–2010. Must we not ask ourselves a simple but critical question: is history repeating itself? Lessons were learned from the events of October 3–4, 1993 that were profoundly important to the military to make it better operationally and tactically. There were also many political decisions made regarding Somalia in 1993 that should have taught those decision-makers some lessons as well. But it seems that they learned few lessons, if any, because the next seven years were marked by political-military decisions of serious and dire consequence, the most egregious of which has been a significant reduction in the size of our Armed Forces.

I believe we have somewhat recovered from many of these negatives of the 1990s, but not completely. Of course, we were then confronted with the terrorist attack on our nation on September 11, 2001, which put us at war in order to protect the people, our freedoms, and our way of life … the *hard right* thing was done.

The time periods in which the most worrisome decision-making has taken place happen to be during Democratic administrations. Presidents Clinton and Obama are exceptionally charismatic men, but charismatic leadership will get you only so far. From the perspective of true leadership experience, I see some with President Clinton who had served as the Governor of Arkansas, but pretty much none with President Obama. As for know-how regarding the challenges of crisis leadership, I see little to none for both. A leader who suffers from this kind of inexperience should always be surrounded by highly qualified, competent, experienced people in key positions; both Presidents failed here as well. For instance, President Clinton's Secretary of Defense, the late Les Aspin, resigned due to his significant failures, and the Attorney General, Janet Reno, was responsible for the fiasco in Waco, Texas at the compound of the Branch Davidian cult. In the case of President Obama's administration, you see Chief of Staff Rahm Emanuel choosing to leave his important position after less than two years to pursue the very personal goal of running for the office of mayor of Chicago. This lack of commitment to President Obama and the administration is a sign that personal gain is of top priority to Emanuel. These two Presidents fit the mold of very likeable, popular leaders who want to appease everyone all the time—political correctness is their standard.

Both are also totally inexperienced in the critical role of Commander-in-Chief because neither has had military service of any nature; their military decisions are more often based on political concerns than military success.

Additionally, both Presidents have suffered from a lack of patriotism—President Clinton was a draft dodger in the 1960s as well as a war protester; President Obama supported an anti-American preacher for over twenty years, and chose to apologize to the Muslim world for the actions of the United States of America, to which I can say: he does not need to apologize for anything I have done in serving our great nation.

Focusing on political correctness to a fault often results in a dire failure in decision-making that leads to doing the *easy wrong* thing versus the *hard right* thing. Witness President Clinton's failure to let the mission in Somalia be completed. Witness again President Obama's actions after the horrific terrorist shooting by a Muslim at Ford Hood, Texas, which killed thirteen great Americans, after which the President told America, "Let's not jump to conclusions."

Finally, both Presidents have brought embarrassment to their office. President Clinton's ethical and moral shortcomings are widely recognized, as are President Obama's disrespectful actions toward the Queen of England and his bowing to the King of Saudi Arabia and the Emperor of Japan. Yet another embarrassment occurred when he chose not to observe the customary ritual of saluting a Medal of Honor recipient—SSG Salvatore Giunta, the first living recipient of the Medal since the Vietnam War.

We need to stop this destructive influence by becoming leaders in all aspects of our lives as Americans. If we do not, our country may be destroyed by political correctness alone. God Bless You All.

# Afterword

This book has not been written by a professional author but by a professional soldier who fought the enemy in the streets of Mogadishu, Somalia in Sep–Oct 1993. Furthermore, I was privileged to do so alongside the most professional military personnel I have ever served with in my career. The book is about the importance of leadership and decision-making in tough times, as well as about the amazing battle of October 3–4, 1993, in Somalia. However, most important to me, it has been written with the intent to honor those who fought the fight, and especially to pay a very special tribute of respect to those who made the ultimate sacrifice and gave their all for their comrades and their country.

It is also important to remember respectfully the loved ones of those who did not make it home alive. After my return to the states, I met the families of my six Rangers who I was not able to bring back home safely. I assured each of these families that their loved one would "Never Be Forgotten" as long as I was living. I have kept my word to them and will continue to do so. I visit my six fallen heroes at their resting places very, very often, and I have remained in contact with many of the family members like the families of Dominick Pilla and Jamie Smith. On the 15th anniversary of the October 3, 1993 battle, my wife Linda and I made a very special journey to honor my fallen Rangers. It started at Fort Bliss, Texas on October 2, 2008 and ended in Rehobeth, Massachusetts on October 6.

My Ranger heroes were visited as follows:

SGT Lorenzo Ruiz, Ft. Bliss, TX, Oct 2;

CPL Jamie Smith, Ft. Benning, GA, Oct 3;

SGT Casey Joyce, Arlington National Cemetery, Oct. 4;

SPC Richard Kowalewski, Arlington National Cemetery, Oct. 4;

SGT Dominick Pilla, Vineland, NJ, Oct 5;

CPL James Cavaco, Rehobeth, MA, Oct 6.

At each resting place, I left a black rock signed in gold as follows: their name, "Never Forgotten, COL Danny McKnight, RLTW!"

I have on occasion looked back and wondered if I did somehow fail my Rangers on that October 3rd day in 1993—could I have done something differently to change the outcome? Could I have done more? It has been difficult to self-analyze, but my answer is always "I did not fail them." We all fought a good, brave, and honorable fight. I am proud to say I was leading the Rangers in the streets of Mogadishu in October 1993. Others may choose to judge me differently, and if so, that is their choice. I had the great privilege to be the Ranger Battalion Commander for the Ranger forces of Task Force RANGER, and it was the greatest honor of my career to lead them in combat. The Valorous Unit Award was presented to 3rd Ranger Battalion on August 19, 1996 at Fort Benning, Georgia.

The Battalion had truly distinguished itself by gallantry in action under the most austere and challenging circumstances in Mogadishu. The Rangers of 3rd Battalion were subsequently awarded five Silver Stars, thirty-nine Bronze Stars w/V for Valor, and twenty-six Bronze Stars.

Additionally, I had the great privilege to serve with the extraordinary members of SFOD-D and TF160 SOAR, truly men who were the best of the best in their respective professional areas of expertise. To go to battle with men like MSG Gary Gordon and SFC Randy Shughart is an indescribable honor. These two men truly gave their all for their fellow soldiers and were posthumously honored as recipients of the Medal of Honor for their heroic actions at the Super Six Four crash site and for saving Mike Durant's life. Another very special opportunity was to serve as a combat leader with superiors like MG Garrison and COL Boykin, two of the finest in our professional Armed Forces. It was also an incredible experience to serve with fellow commanders like LTC Tom Matthews and LTC Gary Harrell.

★   ★   ★   ★

There are many personal stories that live on even today for members of Task Force RANGER. One very personal memory for me is that of SGT Ruiz who was killed on October 3, 1993. I recall the World Series game played between the Philadelphia Phillies and the Toronto Blue Jays on October 2nd. It just so happened we were able to watch some live TV via satellite. In the late innings of that game there were two people still awake watching it—me and SGT Ruiz. There we sat watching this World Series game and chatting about anything and everything from the game to family to what the next operation might be like. This time will always be a special memory for me.

Some things of interest occurred during the deployment to Somalia for every element of the Task Force. One of the interesting occurrences for 3rd Ranger Battalion centered on the scheduled September 24, 1993 Ranger Ball. After arriving in Somalia this became an obvious issue to be dealt with. After some discussion with my Battalion Executive Officer I decided to postpone the Ball until February 1994, well after our return in late October. The really interesting facet of this occurrence related to the wine glasses that every attendee gets to take as a keepsake from the Ball; they were already done and were so inscribed with the date of September 24, 1993. They were also the ones used at the February 1994 Ranger Ball. Everyone thought them unique and a very special keepsake, to put it mildly.

*   *   *   *

One final event of note for Task Force RANGER occurred on November 11, 1993 in Washington, D.C.—Veterans Day, after our return from Somalia. Twenty-six soldiers from Task Force RANGER (myself and five other Rangers included) and some from the 10th Mountain Division's QRF comprised a special group that was invited to the White House for Veterans Day activities—not the kind of invitation you turn down. It is a very unfortunate situation when you have the opportunity to visit with the President in the White House and do not feel great about it. The general attitude of the Task Force RANGER soldiers was not especially positive; they considered it to be a duty to attend, but no one was too excited about it. They felt betrayed by these leaders who now wanted to recognize them, but who had not been willing to make the *hard right* decision to complete the mission in Somalia. It seemed to be a token gesture at best, and most certainly was a politically correct one.

On Veterans Day morning we attended a breakfast in the White House, a special time we shared with veterans from WWII, Korea and Vietnam—neither the President nor the Vice President was in attendance. It was a true privilege to be in the White House with these veterans of the past and shaking the hands of these heroic American patriots, and will always be a highlight of my life. When breakfast concluded we moved through a receiving line where we met the President and First Lady. I was a little surprised when I stood in front of President Clinton in the receiving line and had to tell him who I was and what I did in the Army; I thought he might have known a little something about the Ranger Battalion Commander he had committed to combat, but that turned out to be a bad assumption.

After the receiving line was finished, the President moved to a room where all the Veterans Day guests were assembled for his remarks, which included specific recognition of the veterans from WWII, Korea, Vietnam and Somalia. Upon conclusion of his remarks, our group of Somalia veterans proceeded to the Oval Office for a private session with the President, the Secretary of Defense, and the Chairman of the Joint Chiefs of Staff. This entailed meeting these people and a question/answer time with the President in which he asked some general questions related to the events in Somalia. One of his questions related to our working with the United Nations. My answer to President Clinton was generally as follows:

We can work *with* the United Nations and must be able to do so because it will always be there, and its success as an organization will require our participation and support. However, we must never be required to work *for* it.

I then explained that working *for* them meant that they made the decisions, whereas working *with* them meant we were an important part of that process. The President said he did not really understand what I was telling him. I then explained the security issue that had occurred in Mogadishu regarding the UN Forces at the airfield. I specifically explained the incident that involved UN soldiers not returning fire at enemy personnel because they had no ammunition for their weapons while in a security position. The President's response was to ask General Shalikashvili, Chairman of the Joint Chiefs of Staff, "Did that really happen?" The General responded, "Yes, Sir, I believe I recall that occurring."

This was not reassuring. My Commander-in-Chief had just questioned what I said—as if I might lie to him, especially in front of my superiors, my peers, and my subordinates. I would never do such a thing to disrespect the Office of the President of the United States. In my mind he had actually questioned my integrity and disrespected everything I stood for as a member of the United States Armed Forces. My internal reaction was one of disgust and disappointment while my external reaction required me to maintain my composure, which I somehow did. However, I must be perfectly honest and say that I have never forgotten it and never will.

★   ★   ★   ★

I have been asked on occasion about any impact the Somalia events might have had on my career. It was significant. As of August 1993, I had already been selected for promotion to Colonel, which turned out to be my last. I was never selected to command a brigade-size unit after my attendance at the U.S. Army War College in 1994-95, unusual indeed for a former Ranger Battalion Commander. Because I never became a brigade commander, any promotion to the next rank of brigadier general was not going to happen, and I believe the negativity associated with the events of October 3–4, 1993 was a strong influence. Still, I have no ill feelings toward the Army or the military which I truly love. I would not change anything that took place during my incredible twenty-eight-plus year journey in the Army because that journey put me where I am today in life, and that is very fine with me.

I suppose there is one change I would make if it were possible, and that is to have somehow found a way to bring my six heroic Rangers back home from Somalia alive. In November 1993, the final memorial service for those six Rangers was held at Fort Benning. It was time to bring some final closure to their sacrifices, if that is truly possible. Here are my words from that memorial service:

"Today we are here to pay tribute to six very special acts of courage, bravery and heroism. Rangers Joyce, Ruiz, Pilla, Smith, Cavaco and Kowalewski are six of the finest, most valorous soldiers I have known in my twenty years of service. They epitomize the Ranger Creed and those who wear the Ranger Scroll on their shoulder. I am privileged and honored to have served beside them. We will miss them always. They will never be forgotten."

\*    \*    \*    \*

My amazing and incredible journey in the U.S. Army ended on January 1, 2002, my first day as a retired Army veteran. However, I am now blessed to be on another special journey as I travel across our great country as a motivational speaker on leadership, patriotism, commitment and homeland security. As this journey takes me from sea to shining sea, I am blessed to maintain contact with many of those who served in Task Force RANGER, especially my Rangers: Todd Blackburn, Jeff Struecker, Matt Eversmann, Keni Thomas, David Floyd, Chris Hardy, Rick Merritt, Bob Gallagher, Sean Watson, Mike Pringle, Joe Harosky, Raleigh Cash, Rob Phipps, Scott Galentine, Clay Othic, Mike Steele, and Craig Nixon, just to name a few. I also remain connected to Task Force RANGER members from SFOD-D and TF 160 SOAR: Jerry Boykin, Gary Harrell, Norm Hooten, John Macejunas, Tom Matthews, Randy Jones and Mike Durant. I will always remember the men of Task Force RANGER—my subordinates, my peers, my superiors, my friends, my brothers-in-arms.

*Streets of Mogadishu* is the epitome of the best and worst of times for soldiers in combat. The numerous and unsurpassed acts of courage, bravery and heroism during those extraordinary hours on the 3rd and 4th of October 1993 will never be forgotten, nor the leadership, commitment, and dedication shown by those in Task Force RANGER. And most of all, let their actions always be a reminder of the sacrifice necessary to protect our liberties and freedoms and the special way of life of our great nation.

It seems fitting to finish this book in the same manner in which Task Force RANGER began each day in Mogadishu, Somalia:

**God bless America,**
**Land that I love,**
**Stand beside her and guide her**
**Thru the night with a light from above;**

**From the mountains, to the prairies,**
**To the oceans white with foam,**
**God bless America,**
**My home, sweet home.**
**God bless America,**
**My home, sweet home.**

# Glossary

**AC-130 Gunship**. Heavily armed fixed wing Air Force aircraft that provides fire support to ground forces, similar to the C-130 Hercules transport aircraft.

**AH-6 Little Bird** . Light assault helicopter that provides support to Special Operations forces and can be armed with a combination of guns and aerial rockets.

**APC**. An armored personnel carrier that carries personnel and provides some fire support.

**Armor**. Generally includes tanks and Bradley fighting vehicles.

**Black Hawk**. MH-60 helicopter, a rotary-wing combat assault aircraft.

**Call Sign**. An encrypted identification for a given individual of a radio-transmitter station, like Uniform 64.

**CCT.** Air Force ground combat forces assigned to special tactics joint air and ground forces.

**Chalk**. Designated troops that constitute a complete aircraft load.

**CSAR**. Combat search and rescue; mission to locate, communicate with, and recover downed air crews and isolated personnel.

**HMMWV**. High mobility, multi-purpose, wheeled vehicle that is generally lightly protected with little to no armor protection.

**JOC.** Joint Operations Center, a headquarters from which a joint force commander would plan, monitor and execute an operation.

**JSOC**. Joint Special Operations Command; a joint headquarters responsible for Special Operations missions as well as various other aspects of special operations, such as training, exercises and equipment.

**KIA**. Killed in action.

**MEDEVAC**. Medical evacuation of casualties concurrent with medical care.

**MG**. Machinegun or machinegunner.

**MH-6 Little Bird** . Light assault helicopter that provides support to Special Operations forces and can carry four personnel for air-land or fast-rope insertion into the enemy area.

**MIA**. Missing in action.

**MK-19**. Vehicular mounted weapon system that fires grenades.

**MRE.** Meal ready to eat; a totally self-contained complete meal designed to be consumed without cooking or heating, standard combat rations for the U.S. Armed Forces.

**Night Stalkers**. Nickname for the 160th Special Operations Aviation Regiment of the U.S. Army.

**NCO.** Noncommissioned officer, a subordinate officer (as a sergeant) appointed from among enlisted personnel.

**PJ.** Air Force pararescue jumper; specially trained personnel qualified to penetrate to the site of an incident (such as a downed aircraft) by land or parachute, render medical aid, accomplish survival methods, and rescue survivors.

**QRF.** Quick reaction force; military force poised to respond on very short notice.

**RPG.** Rocket-propelled grenade; a handheld, shoulder-fired weapon capable of firing an unguided rocket.

**SEAL.** Sea, Air, Land; U.S. Navy special forces.

**Special Forces**. Highly trained military units that conduct specialized operations such as reconnaissance, unconventional warfare, and counterterrorism.

**Special Operations**. Use of small units in direct or indirect military actions focused on strategic or operational objectives; require units with combinations of trained specialized personnel, equipment and tactics that exceed the routine capabilities of conventional military units.

**TF.** Task force; a temporary unit or formation established to work on a single task.

**UN**. United Nations.

**UNOSOM II** United Nations Operations Somalia II; the follow-on operational concept applied to Somalia after the initial humanitarian mission (UNOSOM I).

**WIA** Wounded in action.

# ARMY RANK STRUCTURE

## Officers

| | |
|---|---|
| 2LT/1LT | 2nd or 1st Lieutenant |
| CPT | Captain |
| MAJ | Major |
| LTC | Lieutenant Colonel |
| COL | Colonel |
| BG | Brigadier General |
| MG | Major General |
| LTG | Lieutenant General |
| GEN | General |

## Enlisted

| | |
|---|---|
| PVT | Private E-1/E-2 |
| PFC | Private First Class |
| SPC | Specialist |
| CPL | Corporal (NCO) |
| SGT | Sergeant (NCO) |
| SSG | Staff Sergeant (NCO) |
| SFC | Sergeant First Class (NCO) |
| MSG | Master Sergeant (NCO) |
| 1SG | First Sergeant (NCO) |
| SGM | Sergeant Major (NCO) |
| CSM | Command Sergeant Major (NCO) |

# Acknowledgements

The American soldier is one of the most respected treasures of our great nation. It is the soldier who has and always will ensure our right to life, liberty, and the pursuit of happiness. As Americans we should always acknowledge and never forget a simple truism that we are the home of the free *because* of the brave. Thank you to all those who have served and are serving in the Armed Forces of the United States of America, as well as all those who will choose to do so in the future.

I wrote this book in order to provide another perspective on the story of Task Force RANGER in Mogadishu, Somalia from August to October 1993. It is important to understand that my perspective is limited in some ways, as I am simply just a part of the total story. Most important, I wanted to pay tribute to all those who were part of the events reflected in this writing. Furthermore, I am so thankful for all those who enabled me to survive in the streets of Mogadishu. Above all, I must thank God for watching over me and allowing me to live through that battle. He truly had a plan that said, *I am not finished with Danny McKnight on earth quite yet*. This I know to be true because of the blessings I am able to share with others in our country today, those of sacrifice, love, patriotism, family, and God's greatness.

To all the wonderful family I am blessed to have in my life— Linda, my loving wife and best friend, you were a special part of making this book happen. You were supportive of my efforts and knew when I needed encouragement to reach the finish line. You were also the BEST critic of my writing as you read and typed every single word of it, somehow reading and making sense of all my handwritten pages. To my parents and two brothers, thanks for putting up with me for the past sixty years; your love and support have made me what I am today. To my in-laws, Virginia and Iner, thank you for sharing your Linda with me as well as loving me so much. Also, a special thanks to you for proofreading every word on every page before it was forwarded to the publisher—editors had an easy job after your proofing was done. Last but not least, the kids in my life today who brighten each and every day for me—my daughters Robin and Pam, my stepdaughter Katie, my stepson Tim, grandchildren Dylan, Jared, Macen and Olivia.

I want to thank the American people for their support and friendship as I have traveled across the country as a motivational speaker; you have inspired me more than you will ever realize. A special thank you to the many veterans of our military whom I have been privileged to meet and be inspired by along the way:  I am honored to be among your ranks. Two more very noteworthy people who are my good friends as well are George Dodson and August Vernon. George and his wife Katie are not only my publishers, but have become good friends who offered lots of sound advice over the past few years. Thanks for letting me do this book pretty much my way.

August is a professional operations officer and personal friend who made one very significant recommendation to me. He recommended that I contact his publisher friend, George Dodson, about publishing my book; August, thank you very much.

Special thanks to Adam Davies. This brilliant young man with literary editing experience contacted me in July 2010 for assistance with some military writing he was doing for another project. Months later Adam became the editor for *Streets of Mogadishu*. His professionalism and commitment as the editor brought this book to a successful conclusion. I would also like to thank Mary Hogan Hearle who masterfully edited the final manuscript.

Thank you also to all the men and women I was privileged to serve with during my many years in the U.S. Army: my superiors, my peers, my subordinates. Thanks for your leadership, commitment, dedication and friendship. I will always have a very thankful respect for those who serve in the 75th Ranger Regiment, and especially those in 3rd Ranger Battalion. Rangers Lead the Way!

Three men who were special in my Ranger career are Glen Bloomstrom, David Moran and Jeff Struecker. These men are Army Chaplains who served with me at some point in 3rd Ranger Battalion. Glen was the 3rd Ranger Battalion Chaplain when I was the Executive Officer, and we participated in Operation JUST CAUSE in 1989. David was the 3rd Ranger Battalion Chaplain when I was the Battalion Commander, and deeply involved in the events associated with the actions of Somalia in October 1993. Jeff was an infantry Staff Sergeant in the streets of Mogadishu with me in 1993, became an Army Chaplain in 2000 and retired from the Army in 2011. To all three, thanks for your special blessings along the way.

My final thank you is to the members of Task Force RANGER

and their loved ones. To my Task Force comrades, you all are my special heroes! Thank you for the privilege of serving with you, especially in combat. Your courage, bravery, sacrifice and professionalism will never be forgotten. To the wives, the mothers, the fathers, the brothers, the sisters and the children: thank you—your love and support was so very important each and every day to your soldier.

To our great nation, thank you for the freedoms we enjoy. One nation under God, indivisible with liberty and justice for all. Let it never be forgotten that …

**It's the Soldier who salutes the flag,**
**Who serves beneath the flag,**
**And whose coffin is draped by the flag**

# About the Author

**COLONEL DANNY R. MCKNIGHT**
**U.S. Army (Retired)**

 Colonel Danny R. McKnight was a distinguished military graduate from Florida State University in 1973. He graduated with a B.S. in Management, then completed the Infantry Officer Basic Course, Airborne and Ranger Schools.

Colonel McKnight was assigned to the Mountain Ranger Camp in March 1974 where he served as a Company Executive Officer and Instructor. Upon completion of the Infantry Officer Advance Course, he served in Korea as a Battalion Adjutant and was Aide-De-Camp to the Commanding General, 2d Infantry Division. Following this tour, COL McKnight returned to Fort Benning where he served as Aide-De-Camp for the same General Officer who was the Commanding General at Fort Benning. While at Fort Benning, he was assigned to the 1st Battalion 58th Infantry (Mech) where he commanded Company C for 22 months. Next, he was assigned as an Assistant Professor of Military Science at the University of Florida ROTC Department. While at the university,

COL McKnight earned his Masters Degree in Higher Education and Administration. He then attended Air Command and Staff College at Maxwell Air Force Base, Alabama. Following this, COL McKnight returned to Fort Benning where he served as the Adjutant, 75th Ranger Regiment; S3, 3d Battalion, 14th Infantry; S5, 75th Ranger Regiment; Executive Officer, 3d Battalion, 75th Ranger Regiment; and Executive Officer, 75th Ranger Regiment. He departed Fort Benning for Schofield Barracks, Hawaii where he commanded 4-27th Infantry for 19 months. Upon his return from Hawaii, he assumed command of 3d Ranger Battalion on 11 February 1993 where he commanded for 17 months. He then attended the U.S. Army War College at Carlisle Barracks, PA. After graduation from the War College, he was assigned as the Senior Adviser at the 29th Infantry Division, Fort Belvoir, VA. He then assumed duties as the Deputy Chief of Staff, Training, First U.S. Army, Fort Gillem, GA for 2 ½ years. His final assignment was as the Chief of Staff, First U.S. Army, serving for 19 months before retiring on January 1, 2002.

Colonel McKnight's awards and decorations include the Legion of Merit (2OLC), the Bronze Star Medal W/V Device, the Purple Heart, the Meritorious Service Medal (5OLC), the Army Commendation Medal (1OLC), the Army Achievement Medal, the National Defense Service Medal w/Bronze Star, the Armed Forces Expeditionary Medal w/Arrowhead and Bronze Star, the Combat Infantryman's Badge, the Ranger Tab, The Master Parachutist Badge w/Bronze Star and the Pathfinder Badge.

Colonel McKnight and his wife Linda reside in Rockledge, Florida.

# RESOURCES

The primary source for this book without question is me, Danny Ray McKnight. This is because what I have chosen to share with everyone I based on my personal perspective as I saw things. My leadership position as the Commander of 3rd Ranger Battalion allowed me to participate in the decision-making process for Task Force RANGER at the planning and execution levels. Furthermore, my position as the Convoy Commander on the operations in Somalia gave me a detailed look at how the operations were executed from beginning to end. My personal knowledge has been significantly enhanced through many discussions with other members of Task Force RANGER, most especially my Rangers who were there. These discussions took place both in Mogadishu and after our return to the states, and some even since my retirement. Also, some of my opinions and beliefs as expressed in the book are based on research as well as discussion with people outside of Task Force RANGER. As I stated previously, this book was not intended to be another *Black Hawk Down*, but rather an additional perspective that would provide the rest of the story.

Other generally contributing sources are as follows:

BOOKS

Bowden, Mark. *Black Hawk Down*. New York: Atlantic Monthly Press, 1999.

ARTICLES

"The Raid That Went Wrong," Rick Atkinson, The Washington Post, January 30, 1994. An account of the battle from both the American and Somali viewpoints.

"Iraqi Documents Show Saddam Possessed WMD, Had Extensive Terror Ties," Scott Wheeler, CNSNews.com, October 4, 2004. Documents that reveal numerous efforts by Saddam Hussein's regime to work with terror organizations to target Americans like in Somalia.

Declaration of Independence and Constitution of the United States of America.

# NOTES

1. The Korean Demilitarized Zone (DMZ) is a strip of land, one hundred sixty miles long and approximately two and a half miles wide that serves as a buffer between North and South Korea. It is the most heavily militarized border in the world today. Owing to the genuine hostility between the North and the South, large numbers of soldiers from both sides patrol inside the DMZ, but they are officially prohibited from crossing the Military Demarcation Line (MDL) that goes down the center of the DMZ. Sporadic outbreaks of violence due to North Korean hostilities have killed over five hundred South Korean soldiers and fifty U.S. soldiers along the DMZ since 1953. The North Korean government has never acknowledged direct responsibility for any of the incidents and incursions. I was in Korea as the Aide to then Major General Grange when the third infiltration tunnel was discovered. Page 26.

2. The Best Ranger Competition was created to identify the best two-man Ranger "buddy" team in the Army; the competition has evolved over the past years to include competitors from the entire U.S. Armed Forces. The objective was simple and clear from the start—competition should place extreme demands on the teams' physical, mental and technical abilities as Rangers. The standards of performance must vastly exceed those required of the average soldier. The competition is a three-day event consisting of physical and mental tasks undertaken with very little rest between events. Selected events must be completed to remain in the competition. Page 27.

3. Justice was served to some degree on May 1, 2011 when 24
   Navy SEALS of the United States Armed Forces Special Oper-
   ations Command conducted an assault on the compound of
   Osama bin Laden in Pakistan. Osama bin Laden, the leader of
   Al-Qaida, was killed along with several others who were pro-
   tecting him. The mission to capture or kill Bin Laden was suc-
   cessful, and the world's number one terrorist was dead.
   Page 172.